THE ACOUSTIC GUITAR METHOD

COMPLETE EDITION

by DAVID HAMBURGER

This edition contains books 1, 2, and 3 bound together in one easy-to-use volume

Cover photograph: Rory Earnshaw

Book 1 photographs: page 8 (center), Donald Kallaus; page 18, Frank Driggs Collection; page 36, courtesy Country Music Foundation; page 37 Scott Newton/*Austin City Limits*; page 43, Jeffery Pepper Rodgers; all other photos by Christopher Maas, Trpti Todd, and Andrew DuBrock

Book 2 photographs: pages 59, 61, 76, 80, Barbara Gelfand

Book 3 photographs: pages 96, 104, 109, 114, 122, 127, Christopher Maas; page 103, courtesy Pat Travis Eatherly; page 132, Todd Wolfson

ISBN 1-890490-55-5

STRING LETTER PUBLISHING

Visit Hal Leonard Online at
www.halleonard.com

In Australia Contact:
Hal Leonard Australia Pty. Ltd.
22 Taunton Drive P.O. Box 5130
Cheltenham East, 3192 Victoria, Australia
Email: ausadmin@halleonard.com

MUSIC NOTATION KEY

The music in this book is written in standard notation and tablature. Here's how to read it.

Standard notation is written on a five-line staff. Notes are written in alphabetical order from A to G.

The duration of a note is determined by the note head, stem, and flag. A whole note (○) equals four beats. A half note (♩) is half of that: two beats. A quarter note (♩) equals one beat, and an eighth note (♪) equals half of one beat.

Rests indicate places where you don't play. A whole-note rest (-) lasts for four beats, a half-note rest (-) lasts for two beats, a quarter-note rest (𝄽) lasts for one beat, and an eighth-note rest (𝄾) lasts for half a beat.

The fraction (4/4, 3/4, 6/8, etc.) shown at the beginning of a piece of music denotes the time signature or rhythmic pulse of the music. The top number tells you how many beats are in each measure, and the bottom number indicates the rhythmic value of each beat (4 equals a quarter note, 8 equals an eighth note, and 2 equals a half note). The most common time signature is 4/4, which signifies four quarter notes per measure. Waltz time, 3/4, has three quarter notes per measure.

Repeat symbols are placed at the beginning and end of the passage to be repeated.

You should ignore repeat symbols with the dots on the right side the first time you encounter them; when you come to a repeat symbol with dots on the left side, jump back to the previous repeat symbol facing the opposite direction (if there is no previous symbol, go to the beginning of the piece). The next time you come to the repeat symbol, ignore it and keep going unless it includes instructions such as "Repeat three times."

In tablature, the six horizontal lines represent the six strings of the guitar, with the first string on the top and sixth on the bottom. The numbers tell you which fret to play on the given string. Tablature does not indicate rhythm values for the notes, so refer to the notation to know how long to play each note.

Chord diagrams show where the fingers go on the fingerboard. Frets are shown horizontally, and the thick top line represents the nut. The sixth (lowest-pitched) string is on the far left, and first (highest-pitched) string is on the far right. Dots show where the fingers go, and the numbers above the diagram tell you which fretting-hand fingers to use: 1 for the index finger, 2 the middle, 3 the ring, 4 the pinky, and T the thumb. An X indicates a string that should be muted or not played; 0 indicates an open string.

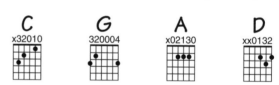

In strumming patterns, pick direction is shown with arrows: downstrokes are toward the floor, upstrokes toward the ceiling.

It might seem strange that an arrow pointing up indicates a downstroke and an arrow pointing down indicates an upstroke. Strums are written this way to be consistent with the notation and tablature, in which the lowest-pitched notes are at the bottom and highest-pitched notes are on top.

For single notes played with a pick, these symbols are used for downstrokes and upstrokes:

■ = *downstroke*   V = *upstroke*

CONTENTS – Book 1

CONTENTS – Book 2

CONTENTS – Book 3

WELCOME

Author David Hamburger.

Introduction

The *Acoustic Guitar Method* teaches you how to play guitar using the techniques and songs of American roots music. Beginning with a few basic chords and strums, you'll start right in learning real music drawn from blues, folk, country, and bluegrass traditions. Working in both standard music notation and a special system for guitar called *tablature,* you'll learn how to find notes on the fingerboard by using them in particular song arrangements. You'll use different kinds of picking patterns and expand your collection of chords by learning songs in various keys. And as your knowledge of the fingerboard expands, you'll solidify that knowledge by picking out the melodies to the tunes you're working on. When you're done with the *Acoustic Guitar Method,* you'll know dozens of the tunes that form the backbone of American music and be able to play them using a variety of flatpicking and fingerpicking techniques.

WHY ACOUSTIC GUITAR?

The acoustic guitar is an incredibly flexible instrument. With just a few chords under your fingers you can play dozens of traditional and popular tunes; with time and effort, you can take the same instrument to virtuosic heights. The acoustic guitar knows few stylistic limits: everything from Lester Flatt's bluegrass backup to John Hurt's country blues fingerpicking, from the Everly Brothers' percussive rock strumming to Leo Kottke's supercharged slide workouts, has been done on essentially the same instrument. You can make music on an acoustic guitar all by yourself or use it as a songwriting tool, and since you can play both rhythm and lead, it's a great instrument for bands and jamming as well.

The amount and variety of music that's made on the acoustic guitar is staggering. Country, blues, bluegrass, jazz, folk, rock—acoustic guitar lies at the heart of all these styles. You may find yourself wanting to check out a little bit of everything. Or maybe one style will grab your attention and not let go. No matter where your interests lead you, you'll be expanding your ears, strengthening your fingers, and learning more about music and your instrument.

WHY ROOTS MUSIC?

The various genres collectively referred to as *roots music* are all very much alive, and the guitar is very much a part of those traditions. Whether you're revved up about learning fingerstyle blues, bluegrass flatpicking, basic country backup, or western swing, it all starts with the same fundamentals. Learning tunes is a practical and fun way to acquire a chord vocabulary, practice strumming techniques, learn about picking and playing single notes, and apply picking patterns to real-world situations.

We've chosen the traditional tunes in this series for their variety and accessibility and because they are great songs and a blast to play. These songs are survivors

Need help with the lesson material in this book? Ask a question in our free, online support forum in the Guitar Talk section of www.acousticguitar.com.

and have become the common currency within their respective genres. When people get together to play, these tunes provide a meeting place for musicians of varied backgrounds and levels of experience.

Some of these songs may also be familiar to you from various pop sources. Musicians have always borrowed, updated, and rearranged older material, but as the folk-revival students of the 1950s came of age in the 1960s, many of them brought what they had learned about earlier styles of music into the pop mainstream. So as you learn and play these songs, you're not only walking in the footsteps of Mississippi John Hurt and the Carter Family, Leadbelly and Doc Watson, you may find yourself learning something Bob Dylan once learned, singing a melody Bonnie Raitt once sang, pondering a lyric Jerry Garcia once pondered. Because so many people have continued to learn and play these songs, dipping into them may also illuminate the work of contemporary songwriters such as Gillian Welch and David Rawlings, Steve Earle, and Lucinda Williams. In time, these songs may provide points of departure for your own songwriting.

In these pages you'll find background on roots-music styles and lists of recordings where you can hear how musicians, past and present, have interpreted and reinvented these songs. Follow these trails to a wealth of great music and artists, as you discover the joy of hearing these essential American tunes come to life in your own hands.

Let's go over some essentials about your guitar, take a look at how it works, and discuss how to tune it.

YOU AND YOUR GUITAR

By and large the sound of American roots music and its many branches is the sound of the steel-string guitar, whether strummed, soloed on, or fingerpicked. Crisp bluegrass backup, bluesy riffs, reflective fingerstyle instrumentals, gritty and evocative slide work, triumphant rock strumming—if any of that is what's gotten you into the guitar, chances are you want to play a steel-string instrument. You can do all the same things (with the exception of slide) on a nylon-string guitar; the instrument will just sound and respond a little differently.

PARTS OF THE GUITAR

Here's an illustrated guide to the parts of a standard acoustic steel-string guitar, often referred to as a *flattop guitar*. People are going to be talking about these things, and you should know your tuning machines from your pickguard, your bridge from your fingerboard, and so on. So take a glance now, and check back when you come across something you don't understand.

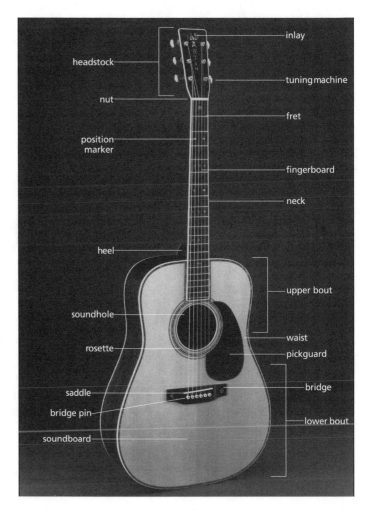

CHOOSING AN INSTRUMENT

The *dreadnought* is the standard acoustic guitar shape, a relatively large, squarish design developed by C.F. Martin around 1916; nearly every guitar company now makes dreadnought-style instruments. There are also numerous smaller-bodied instrument styles, often based on older designs by Martin or Gibson and variously referred to as *parlor, concert,* or simply *small-bodied* guitars. These are often easier to hold and to wrap your arms around as a beginner than the bulkier dreadnought or the equally large *jumbo* instruments based on Gibson's various models of that name. Different styles and shapes of instruments do sound different from one another, but right now the most important issue is comfort, so get something that feels like it fits your body.

While we're on the subject, keep in mind that you can make music on any instrument. Many musicians use a variety of guitars over the course of their lives or keep a few instruments to change their sound on stage, in the studio, or at home. Much of the earliest country and blues music was made with whatever instruments were available or affordable at the time. People played cheap Stella, Harmony, or hand-me-down guitars because that's what they had, and they made music that's still worth listening to decades later.

In our own era, there are more and more good, inexpensive guitars being produced all the time, making it easier than ever to find a comfortable, reasonably priced, good-sounding beginner instrument. Whether you get something new or secondhand, have the shop where you buy it or a recommended repair shop do a setup before you get started. That basically means adjusting the neck for the most comfortable action, or distance between the strings and the fretboard, putting on a fairly light gauge of strings, and checking the *intonation* (that is, making sure your guitar plays in tune all the way up the neck), which may involve adjustments to the saddle and/or the nut. (Aren't you glad you looked over that illustration on page 5?)

HOLDING THE GUITAR

The standard sitting pose for playing acoustic guitar has the guitar resting on your right leg. Your right arm can drape over the lower bout of the guitar, with the instrument fitting snugly in the crook of your arm. That should leave your right hand dangling somewhere between the bridge and the soundhole, or right at the soundhole's edge, when you go to strum or pick. If you're planning to stand up, you might want to have a strap button attached to the heel of the neck. It doesn't have the same Woody Guthrie–esque hobo look as tying a piece of string around the headstock, but it centers the guitar's body on you a bit better and ensures a more stable placement of the instrument.

Keep your left-hand thumb along the back of the neck, wherever it feels most comfortable. It can creep up over the top, past the fingerboard, as long as it's not actually touching the low string and keeping it from ringing out when you strum. Be sure to keep your fingers arched, with each joint bent; if they flatten out across the strings they will also flatten the sound when you strum.

The standard sitting position.

A strap tied to the headstock (demonstrated by old-time guitar master Norman Blake).

Good thumb position behind the neck.

HOLDING THE PICK

There are a number of ways to grip the pick. Here's one standard way, which you can change to suit what's most comfortable to you as you get going.

Start with your four fingers curled loosely together, as if you were holding a broom handle. Place the wide end of the pick on the first joint of your index finger. Now bring your thumb down to hold the pick in place. If you keep your fingers curled like this—not tightly, but in a little group—they'll be out of the way as you strum the strings.

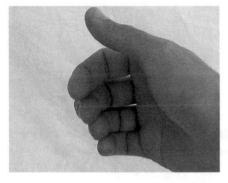 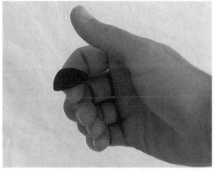 

Start with your fingers curled loosely, place the pick on your index fingertip, and hold it with your thumb.

The thickness (or *gauge*) of the pick you use affects your sound, and the way you grip it affects your ability to get a good strumming sound on both *downstrokes* (toward the floor) and *upstrokes* (toward the ceiling). Try a standard-sized, medium-gauge pick to begin with, and hold it with a moderate grip: tight enough that it doesn't slip out of your hands, but loose enough that you can wobble the tip of the pick back and forth with your other hand.

TUNING UP

Let's try a standard method for getting the guitar in tune to itself. The notes we are tuning to are, from the thickest and lowest-pitched string to the thinnest and highest-pitched one:

Tune-Up
TRACK 2

E	A	D	G	B	E
Sixth	Fifth	Fourth	Third	Second	First

You can hear these open strings on Track 2 of the CD.

You'll need to tune your low E string (meaning your thickest, lowest-pitched one) to some other source first—an E tuning fork, a pitch pipe, a piano, someone else's guitar, or the tune-up track included on the CD. If you're not sure whether a note needs to come up or go down, lower it until you can hear it is definitely too low and then slowly bring it back up. It's easier to hear a note coming up to the correct pitch than down to the correct pitch, and this approach also reduces the chances of breaking a string by accidentally cranking it up far beyond the pitch it was meant for.

Once you have your low E string in tune, fret it at the fifth fret (an A note) and tune the open fifth string to that note. Make sure you press the string down just *behind* the fret—toward the tuners—as shown in the photo at right.

Press each string down right next to the fret.

HIGH OR LOW?

Let's clear up one very common source of confusion about strings. When guitarists refer to their "high," "low," "top," and "bottom" strings, they are talking about the pitch of the strings and not their location in space. So your high/top string is actually closest to the floor, and your low/bottom string is closest to the ceiling. If you can just get used to this little quirk of guitar terminology, it will save you a lot of confusion.

Next, press down the fifth string at the fifth fret and tune the fourth string to that note (A). Then press down the fourth string at the fifth fret and match the open third string to that note (D). Press down the third string at the *fourth* fret and match the open second string to that note (B). Finally, match the open first string to the second string at the fifth fret (an E note). The diagram below summarizes this step-by-step process:

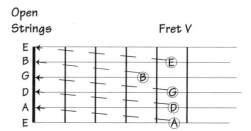

You can also tune each string, one by one, to a pitch pipe, another guitar, or the tuning track on the CD, or else use an electronic tuner. While it's tempting to end the frustration of an out-of-tune guitar as quickly as possible with a tuner, learning to tune up string by string is an important part of developing your ears, and it takes regular practice, just like playing the guitar itself. If you do use a tuner, try to get your guitar at least in the ball park using the fretting method outlined above, and then check your results with the tuner, fixing any out-of-tune strings as you go.

LESSON 1
FIRST CHORDS, FIRST SONG

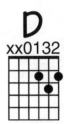

Your first chord is called D.

The diagram at right, variously called a *chord grid* or *diagram* or *frame,* is a graphic representation of your guitar. The strings are the vertical lines, with the thickest and lowest-pitched sixth string on the left and the thinnest and highest-pitched first string on the right. The thick horizontal line is the *nut*—the piece of plastic or bone that holds your strings on the tuner end of the fingerboard. The dots show where you press down the strings, and the numbers indicate which finger to use: 1 for the index, 2 the middle, 3 the ring, and 4 the pinky. The little *X's* mean you don't want to actually play the two lowest strings of the guitar when you play this chord. The little *0* means you do want to hear the open fourth string ring out as part of this chord.

Now, holding your pick, make a series of downstrokes: strumming or dragging the pick across the strings from the fourth, open string, D, through the top string. Tap your foot first, counting "1, 2, 3, 4." Then try strumming down, toward the floor, with each tap of your foot. On paper, we notate that like this:

Every slash stands for a beat, and right now you're playing a strum on every beat. So play a strum for every slash, or four strums.

TROUBLESHOOTING TIPS

"Dave," I hear you say, "that's cool, but my D chord doesn't sound like much. I'm getting maybe two strings to sound, and the rest is all just the futile sound of my pick clicking against the strings with no notes coming out." Well, yes, that's usually how it sounds at first. The lack of sound is mostly about your fretting hand right now, so let's look at a few of the most common snags.

Fingers falling flat. You need to keep your fingers somewhat squared, with your two joints making a box in which the fingerboard is the fourth side. Check on your ring finger in particular: on a D chord it probably wants to flatten out at the first joint, which means it is now muting the high string. That is, even if you're fretting the high string just right, the underside of your ring finger may be muffling it. Squaring up your ring finger should help.

Too far from the fret. "Put your index finger at the second fret" really means, "place your index finger *between* the first fret and the second fret." You don't want to put your finger down on the string right *over* the second fret, but you can't leave it too far back toward the first fret either. The ideal location is about

Too far from the fret.

Too close to the fret.

Just right.

three-quarters of the way toward the second fret. Of course, there will be some variation of finger placement, especially on a chord such as D where more than one finger has to be at the same fret (on different strings) at the same time.

Not pressing down hard enough. This one is tricky. You actually don't need to press down forcefully to make a note sound, and in fact you can build up a lot of unnecessary tension and pain in your hand, not to mention your fingertips, by pressing too hard out of concentration or stress. But you do need to make sure that your effort is evenly distributed over all your fingers in the chord, and if you've already checked for slanted, muffling fingers and how close they are to the right fret, check on how much pressure you're applying to hold down each string.

LEARNING THE SHAPE

Once you've got your chord successfully formed from the diagram, you proba-bly won't ever want to let go of it. But do it anyway; let go and form the chord again. Playing guitar is usually about switching between chords, so while it may seem like a remote possibility right now, what you're aiming for is the ability to form chords without even thinking about which finger is going where. That comes from being able to feel a chord as a single hand position, something to grab all at once.

So if you're sitting around in front of the TV, flipping through a magazine, or sitting on hold on the phone, just keep the guitar right there, with your left hand on the neck. You don't even have to strum—just keep forming a D chord, putting it into place as slowly and carefully as you need to, holding it there for a few seconds, and then letting go. Then do the same thing again. Stop when you get tired of it, put the guitar down, and go do something else for a while (unless you're still on hold).

A

x02130

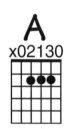

THE A CHORD

Of course, to learn about switching from chord to chord, you'll need to know more than one chord to play. So here's a second chord, A.

You'll have to sort of squish your three fingers together in a little triangle, with your index finger a little further from the second fret than your other two fingers are. It is a violation of our second troubleshooting tip above, since your index finger will be less than three-fourths of the way to the second fret, but you can still make the note on the third string come out clearly, even if your finger is only about halfway between the first and second frets.

Practice this chord the same ways as you did the D chord: hold it down and strum it for a while, tapping your foot and using downstrokes, and also practice just forming and releasing the chord without strumming.

TRACK
④ Ex. 2
A
x02130

THE BIG SWITCH

We're going to switch from one chord to another now. Ready? Play two measures of D (eight downstrokes altogether) followed by two measures of A:

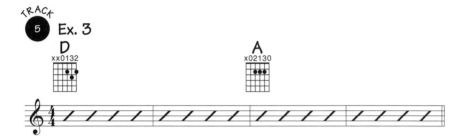

Maybe you had to stop and piece the A chord together. That's cool for now. You can probably hear that if you were actually playing a song, a big pause to put your fingers down one by one on the A would break the flow. We'll deal with that in a minute. But first, just go back and forth between D and A for a while. Don't stop when you're done playing the A—go back and start over with D. That's what those repeat signs (|:) at the beginning and end of the example mean.

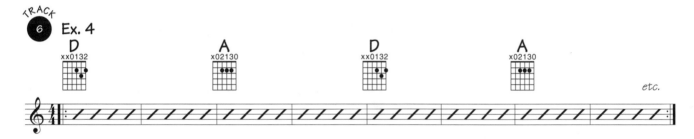

STEP BY STEP

If you're having difficulty with the change, it may help to break it down. The D and the A chord share one note, the second fret on the third string. You use the same finger, your index finger, to play that note in both chords. So when you switch between D and A, you can keep your index finger on the third string as a reference point. Try it:

    1. Form the D chord.

    2. Keeping your index finger down, lift off your middle and ring fingers.

    3. Set your ring finger down on the second fret of the second string.

    4. Set your middle finger down on the second fret of the fourth string.

There's your A.

To switch back to D, reverse the process:

    1. Keeping your index finger down, lift up your middle and ring fingers.

    2. Set your middle finger down on the first string.

    3. Set your ring finger down on the second string, forming the D chord.

FIRST SONG

Now we're ready to play a tune. "Columbus Stockade Blues" became an early country music hit when the duo of Darby and Tarlton recorded it in 1927, and it has been recorded by many other singers since then. You can play the verse knowing just D and A. Note that the melody (the word *way*) starts before the first full measure—this is called a *pickup*.

COLUMBUS STOCKADE BLUES

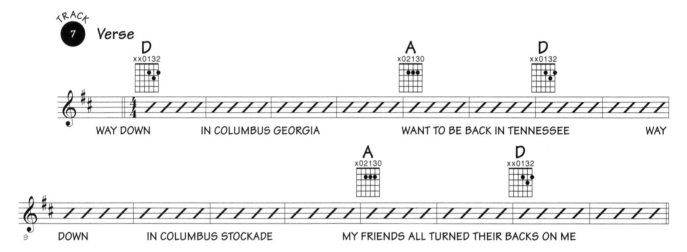

WAY DOWN   IN COLUMBUS GEORGIA   WANT TO BE BACK IN TENNESSEE   WAY

DOWN   IN COLUMBUS STOCKADE   MY FRIENDS ALL TURNED THEIR BACKS ON ME

Congratulations! Even if it sounds a little muffly and weird, you've just played your first song on the guitar.

Slow Train Through Georgia

ESSENTIAL LISTENING

Oklahoma-born Woody Guthrie personified the hobo singer as he rode the rails during the Great Depression, singing about the unmet promises of the American Dream. His tremendous output included such American anthems as "This Land Is Your Land" and "Do Re Mi," and his influence can be clearly traced through the decades since his death in 1967: from Pete Seeger through Bob Dylan, Tom Paxton, Phil Ochs, Guthrie's own son Arlo, and the generations of singer-songwriters who have followed.

Guthrie's extensive repertoire of traditional material included **"Columbus Stockade Blues,"** which can be found on *The Early Years* (Legacy) as well as on recordings by traditional country pickers **Norman Blake** (*Slow Train Through Georgia*, Rounder) and Doc Watson (*Third Generation Blues*, Sugar Hill) and the progressive bluegrass band Chesapeake (*Rising Tide*, Sugar Hill).

The capo is holding the strings down at the second fret.

SINGING TIP

If you find any of these songs hard to sing in the keys we are using, you might want to check out a handy little device called a capo. A capo presses down all the strings at any fret that you choose, raising their pitch without your having to retune. Then you can play the same chord fingerings you already know, but they will *sound* in a different key.

So if "Columbus Stockade Blues," for example, is a little low for your voice as written here, try putting a capo at the second fret. Play the same chord fingerings with the capo and see if that feels better (you're now singing in the key of E instead of D!). You can go higher up the neck, too, if you like.

LESSON 2
NEW CHORD, NEW STRUM

Here's our next chord, E.

Like A and D, E involves keeping three of your fingers all bunched together, this time on the fifth, fourth, and third strings. Spend some time getting familiar with where your fingers go, doing the same forming-and-letting-go exercise you did on the A and D chords. Then, try switching between A and E, playing two measures of each chord at a time:

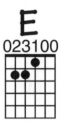

E
023100

TRACK 8 Ex. 1

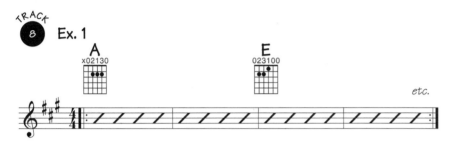

etc.

STEP BY STEP

Switching between A and D, you were able to pivot around the index finger, holding it down while you moved your other fingers around it. You have almost the same situation when you switch between A and E—almost, but not quite. This time, your index finger stays on the third string for both chords, but it doesn't stay at the same fret. Try this step-by-step breakdown to get from A to E:

1. From playing an A chord, lift up your second and third fingers while keeping down your index finger.
2. Slide your index finger back along the string from the second fret to the first fret.
3. Set down your second and third fingers on the second fret of the fourth and fifth strings to complete the E chord.

To switch from E back to A, reverse the process:

1. Lift up your second and third fingers while keeping down your index finger on the third string.
2. Slide your index finger up along the string from the first to the second fret.
3. Set down your middle finger on the second fret of the fourth string, and your third finger on the second fret of the fifth string.

PLAY IT

Now let's turn to our second song. "Careless Love" has had a long life as both a folk and a blues song; in the 1940s it was part of Leadbelly's repertoire. The song rocks back and forth between A and E two times before going up to a D chord in the third line. Strum with all downstrokes, and then we'll talk about a new strum to try.

CARELESS LOVE

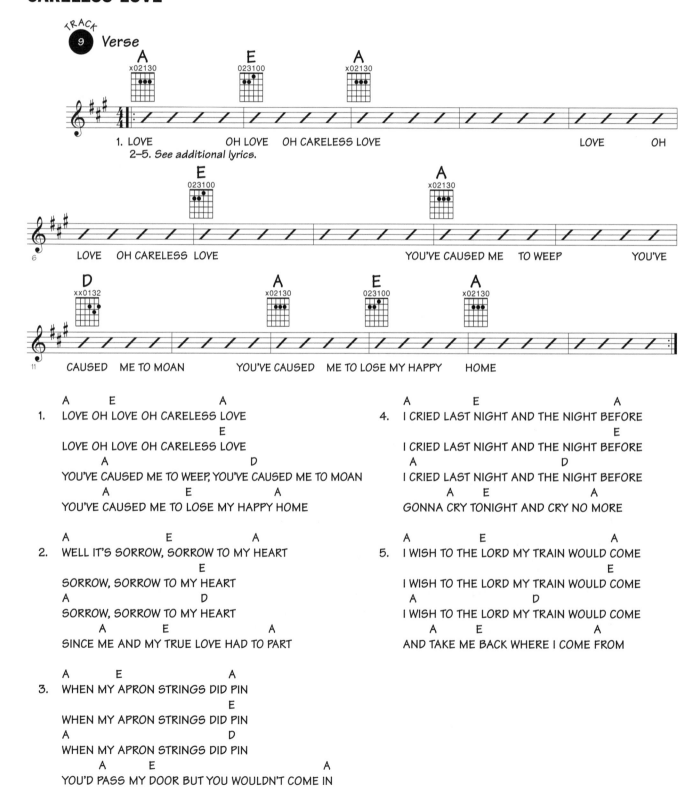

1.
A   E   A
LOVE OH LOVE OH CARELESS LOVE
                            E
LOVE OH LOVE OH CARELESS LOVE
     A   D
YOU'VE CAUSED ME TO WEEP, YOU'VE CAUSED ME TO MOAN
     A   E   A
YOU'VE CAUSED ME TO LOSE MY HAPPY HOME

2.
A   E   A
WELL IT'S SORROW, SORROW TO MY HEART
               E
SORROW, SORROW TO MY HEART
A   D
SORROW, SORROW TO MY HEART
     A   E   A
SINCE ME AND MY TRUE LOVE HAD TO PART

3.
A   E   A
WHEN MY APRON STRINGS DID PIN
                       E
WHEN MY APRON STRINGS DID PIN
A   D
WHEN MY APRON STRINGS DID PIN
                    A   E   A
YOU'D PASS MY DOOR BUT YOU WOULDN'T COME IN

4.
A   E   A
I CRIED LAST NIGHT AND THE NIGHT BEFORE
                                E
I CRIED LAST NIGHT AND THE NIGHT BEFORE
A   D
I CRIED LAST NIGHT AND THE NIGHT BEFORE
          A   E   A
GONNA CRY TONIGHT AND CRY NO MORE

5.
A   E   A
I WISH TO THE LORD MY TRAIN WOULD COME
                                E
I WISH TO THE LORD MY TRAIN WOULD COME
A   D
I WISH TO THE LORD MY TRAIN WOULD COME
          A   E   A
AND TAKE ME BACK WHERE I COME FROM

INTRODUCING UPSTROKES

So far we've done everything with just downstrokes. Now we'll start moving the pick in both directions, using *upstrokes* as well. An upstroke, just as you'd expect, is the opposite of a downstroke: instead of bringing the pick down or toward the floor, bring the pick back up toward yourself. In the following songs, we'll use arrows to indicate down and up strums:

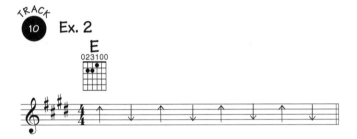

Don't let the directions of the arrows confuse you; they relate to guitar tablature, which we'll discuss in Lesson 3. In the following exercise on an E chord, take things at a slow tempo and practice following every downstroke with an upstroke:

With downstrokes, you can get away with holding the pick as firmly as you like, and you can angle the pick so that it slides easily across the strings. Once you're pulling the pick back up the strings, however, it's a different story. If you continue to hold the pick tightly, you'll get caught in the strings on the upstrokes. Try holding the pick more perpendicularly to the strings, and loosen your grip a little. The pick should give way a little with each string.

If you don't relax your grip, you'll find yourself compensating by changing the entire angle of your hand from the wrist down. This allows the pick to get across the strings on an upstroke but makes for a great deal of extra work, and as you work up to playing faster and more intricate material, all that extra motion will really slow you down. So be flexible with your fingers rather than your wrist, loosening your grip enough to let the pick change angles.

DIFFERENT STROKES

Let's get back to those new strum patterns. Once you can do solid alternating up- and downstrokes, try leaving out the upstroke after the first downstroke (Example 3). For another pattern, leave out the upstroke on the first and third beats (Example 4).

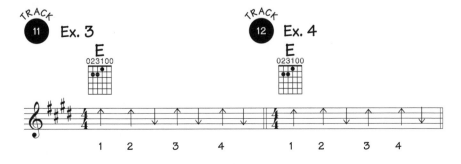

Let's return to "Careless Love" and play it using this last strum.

CARELESS LOVE

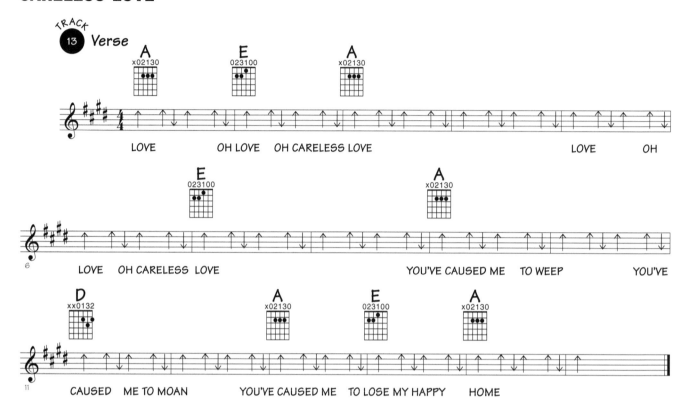

LOVE   OH LOVE   OH CARELESS LOVE   LOVE   OH

LOVE   OH CARELESS LOVE   YOU'VE CAUSED ME   TO WEEP   YOU'VE

CAUSED   ME TO MOAN   YOU'VE CAUSED ME TO LOSE MY HAPPY   HOME

ESSENTIAL LISTENING

Huddie Ledbetter, a farm laborer and a convicted felon, acquired the moniker **Leadbelly** because of his unmatchable stamina and won a pardon from Shaw State Prison Farm by playing his guitar for the governor of Texas. Leadbelly played ebullient and extroverted blues, as well as ballads, field hollers, and other folk songs. In 1933 song researchers John and Alan Lomax secured the singer's release from his second prison sentence. Leadbelly relocated to New York, where he recorded for the Library of Congress and Folkways, becoming best known for the songs "Irene, Goodnight" and "The Midnight Special."

Leadbelly's version of **"Careless Love"** can be heard on *Midnight Special: The Library of Congress Recordings*, Vol. 1 (Rounder). The song has also been recorded by Brownie McGhee (*The Folkways Years*, Smithsonian Folkways), Josh White (*Free and Equal Blues*, Smithsonian Folkways) and more recently, Cephas and Wiggins (*Guitar Man*, Flying Fish/Rounder), as well as many country, folk, and bluegrass artists.

LESSON 3
TAB BASICS AND YOUR FIRST MELODY

Now that you have a few chords and some strumming under your fingers, it's time to play your first melody. Let's go over some basics about the notes on your fingerboard and how they are written out using tablature, and then we'll use this knowledge in a song.

NOTES ON THE FINGERBOARD

All of the notes on the fingerboard are named using one of seven letters: A, B, C, D, E, F, or G. As you know from tuning your guitar, the notes of the open strings are, from the lowest-pitched string to the highest: E, A, D, G, B, and E.

Open
Strings

```
E
B
G
D
A
E
```

If you went up the A string, naming the notes, it would look like this:

```
A     B  C     D     E  F     G     A
```

Notice that B and C are only one fret apart, as are E and F, while all the other notes are two frets apart. In fact that same pattern holds true across the entire fretboard. A distance of one fret is also called a *half step,* and a distance of two frets is also called a *whole step.*

Now, you could start on any string and name the notes on that string based on these half steps and whole steps. If you did, you would end up with something like this:

Open
Strings   Fret XII

As you can see, the basic seven notes keep repeating on different strings and at different frets up the neck. On the guitar, you can often play the same note at several locations: for instance, the A you get at the fifth fret of the sixth string is the same note as the open fifth string. Then the A note at the second fret of the third string is an octave higher—this means it's the same note at a higher frequency. And the A at the fifth fret of the first string is an octave higher still.

TABLATURE BASICS

A common way to notate guitar music is using *tablature,* often called *tab.* Tab works a lot like the fingerboard diagrams above. There are six horizontal lines, one representing each string. Numbers written on those lines tell you at what fret to place your finger, on which string. The bottom line of the tablature is the lowest-pitched (sixth) string of the guitar, and the top line is the highest-pitched (first) string. Take, for example, this little piece of tab:

It means, "put your finger at the second fret on the third string and play that note." As you read it from left to right, the tab shows you what to play over time. For instance, this example tells you what notes to play, and in what order, for the melody of "Jingle Bells":

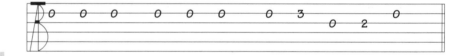

Tab doesn't tell you, though, how long to play each note or how long to wait until you play the next one. For that information, you can use your ears or what's called *standard notation,* as we will see in the next lesson.

GET ALONG

Let's try a melody written out in tab: the old-time tune "Get Along Home, Cindy," also known simply as "Cindy." Look at the tab to see where to put your fingers, and listen to the CD for the rhythms.

GET ALONG HOME, CINDY

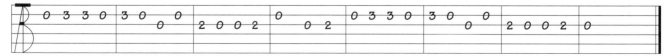

LESSON 4
READING NOTES

Standard music notation, like tab, stretches out in a line to show you what is happening over time. But where tablature shows whether to play a higher or lower string/fret, standard notation tells you whether to play a higher or lower *note*. Plus it shows us when to play each note and how long it rings out. With all this information, we can figure out what a piece of music should sound like even without hearing a recording. So let's go over a few basics about standard notation and then play another melody.

Standard notation is based on the *staff,* which has five lines. Each line of the staff, and each space in between, represents a particular note:

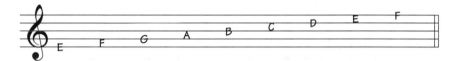

Placing a note symbol on a particular line or space tells you to play that note on the guitar. For example, a note placed on the line for G means, "Play the note G." A note placed in the space for A means, "Play the note A."

Here are the six open strings of the guitar, shown on the staff and in tab:

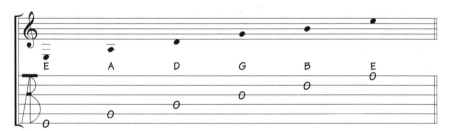

Filling in all the notes from the low string to the high string, we get this:

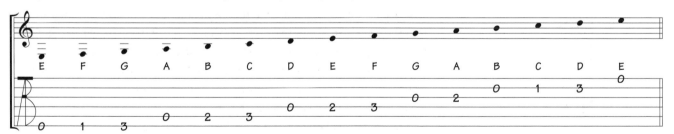

I know what you're thinking. "Dave," you want to say, "this is swell, but what's with the funky little lines below the staff?" Well, those are called *ledger lines.* Each ledger line is like a little piece of an extra line of the staff, running below the regular five lines. They let you show notes on the guitar that go lower than the bottom line of the staff, notes we'll be learning one by one as we go along.

RHYTHM BASICS

Along with the notes themselves, standard notation shows you the rhythms—when to play each note and how long it rings out.

Tap your foot and count along: 1, 2, 3, 4, 1, 2, 3, 4. In this example, one *measure* is the amount of time it takes to count to four. There are four beats, or taps of your foot, in a measure. A *whole note* (𝅝) lasts for all four beats. A *half note* (𝅗𝅥) is half that: two beats. A *quarter note* (♩) equals one beat, and an *eighth note* (♪) equals half a beat. Take a look at these examples and count them out as shown.

TRACK
15
Ex. 1

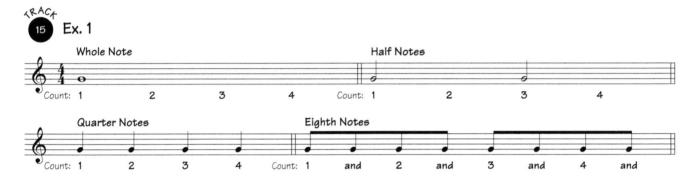

PUTTING IT TOGETHER

Standard notation is definitely more abstract than tablature, but it's still just a graph. Going up or down the lines of the staff tells you to play notes that are higher or lower; going from left to right tells you what order those notes get played in and how long they last. So how does that connect to the actual notes on the fretboard?

Look at the example at left. There's a quarter note on the second line of the staff. The second line of the staff is G; the note is a quarter note. G is the open third string of the guitar. So the example is telling you to play the open third string for one beat.

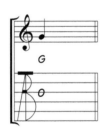

The tab tells you to play the open third string without telling you the name of the note or how long to hold it. The staff tells you the name of the note and for how long to play it. Each system is helpful in its own way. Only guitarists can read tablature, which gives standard notation an edge as a means of communicating with other musicians.

The next example is similar to the G example, but this time, the quarter note is in the second space of the staff, which is A. A is a whole step up from G, or two frets up from the open third string, as the tablature indicates.

Let's read a whole measure. In Example 2 on the next page, each note is a quarter note. Count "1, 2, 3, 4" to yourself, nodding your head or tapping your toe or whatever you like to do. Each note will land on a nod/count/toe tap. Here we are alternating between the G on the open third string and the A on the second fret of the same string.

Now let's try playing eighth notes, which, you remember, happen twice as fast as quarter notes. (What disappears faster from a plate, an eighth of a chocolate-chip cheesecake or a quarter of it?) Count "1 and 2 and 3 and 4 and" and play on all the *ands* as well as the numbers in Example 3, which uses only the open third string.

You may notice that it's starting to get tricky to get your pick back in place from each downstroke to play the next note. Well, the solution is to use a combination of downstrokes and upstrokes to play these single notes, just like we're using a combination of downstrokes and upstrokes to strum chords. In Example 4, play a measure of eighth notes again, and this time, alternate between downstrokes and upstrokes, starting on a downstroke. For single notes, we'll use the symbols at right to indicate downstrokes and upstrokes.

downstroke = ⊓
upstroke = ∨

You can also combine quarter notes and eighth notes in the same measure. Notice that you use a downstroke for each quarter note, followed by a downstroke and an upstroke for each pair of eighth notes. Play Example 5 slowly at first, and remember to count.

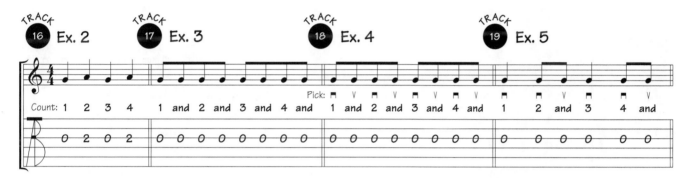

For our next song, you'll need a few more notes: B, D, and E. B, you may recall, is played on the open second string, and it's written on the middle line of the staff. D is the open fourth string, and you can find it just below the bottom line of the staff. And E is a whole step up from D, at the second fret of the fourth string; in notation, it's the bottom line of the staff.

FIDDLIN' ON GUITAR

Let's use all this information in a real melody. "Sally Goodin" is a fiddle tune that has been played by everyone from Doc Watson to western swing bandleader Bob Wills, and those are just the people filed under *W*. As the name implies, fiddle tunes come from the country/bluegrass fiddle tradition, and they are a lot of fun to play on guitar. We'll learn a simple version of the A section now and add in the B section of the song when we get a little further along.

The rhythm is a mixture of quarter and eighth notes, and the count is included beneath the staff to help you keep track. Alternate downstrokes and upstrokes as indicated, and take it slowly at first while you're crossing back and forth between the two strings.

SALLY GOODIN, PART I

AMERICAN
FIDDLE
TUNES

THE LIBRARY OF CONGRESS
ARCHIVE OF FOLK CULTURE

ESSENTIAL LISTENING

Hang around bluegrass pickers for very long and you'll start hearing about **fiddle tunes,** which predate all the hot bluegrass instrumentals such as Earl Scruggs' "Foggy Mountain Breakdown" or Bill Monroe's "Tennessee Blues." Fiddle tunes have their origins in the instrumental and dance pieces brought to the U.S. by early European immigrants, particularly those from the British Isles. They generally adhere to the AABB form: an eight-bar section played twice, followed by a contrasting eight-bar section that is also played twice.

Doc Watson revolutionized the acoustic guitar world in the early '60s with his settings of fiddle tunes on the guitar, a style now called *flatpicking.* Subsequent important flatpickers include Clarence White, Norman Blake, and Tony Rice. You can hear Clarence White play **"Sally Goodin"** on the Kentucky Colonels' *Appalachian Swing!* (Rounder); it's also on the Tony Rice Unit's *Unit of Measure* (Rounder). For an overview of guitarists playing fiddle tunes, check out the compilation *Rounder Bluegrass Guitar.*

LESSON 5
THE G CHORD

Try wrapping your hands around a G chord. This is the first time that the bottom note of the chord, the lowest note you want to hear, isn't actually an open string. So when you're going to form this chord, reach for the low string first—get your ring finger onto the third fret of the sixth string, then put down your middle finger, and finally your pinky. It can be a little tricky to spread your fingers out this much, but laying them down one by one like this can help.

In fact, try this little exercise: Start with a D chord, play four beats, then try to get just your ring finger to the low note of the G chord in time for the next measure (Example 1). Now keep that going, in a loop (Example 2).

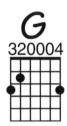

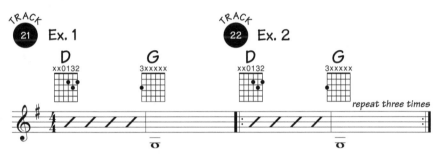

When you're ready, get your middle finger in on the switch as well (Example 3), and then make the full switch (Example 4). Finally, let's *start* on a G and switch to the D (Example 5).

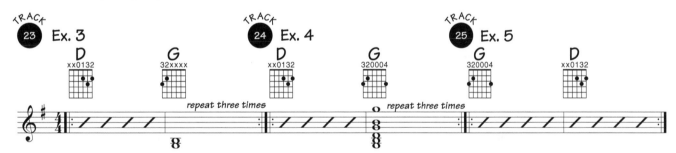

IDA RED

Now let's use that change in a song. "Ida Red" was a staple of western swing-band leader Bob Wills' repertoire and is still played by western swing bands today. Typically this tune has a string of couplet verses that are sung in between instrumental breaks. Try the strum in Example 6. The switch from D back to G at the end of each line is quicker than what we were doing before—only two beats on the D and you're back to G again. You may want to isolate and practice that quick change with the strum. Do it slowly but still in time, as in Example 7.

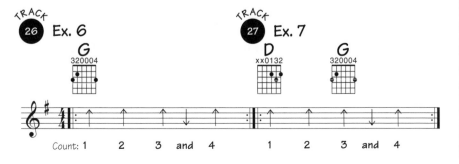

IDA RED

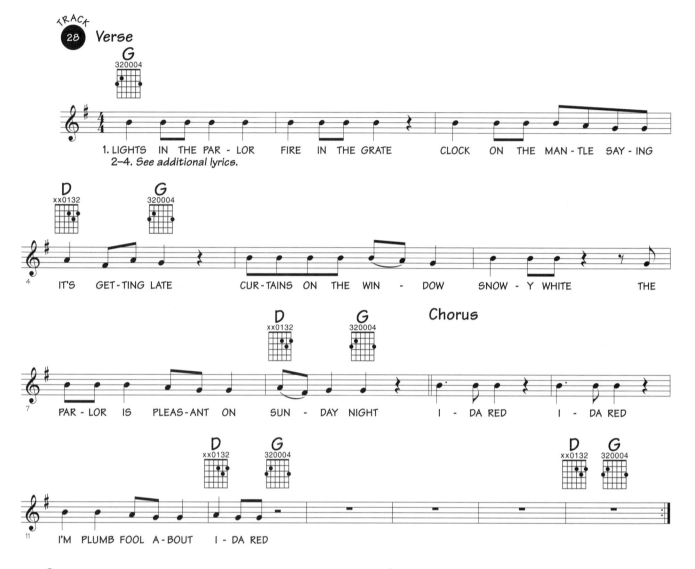

G

1. LIGHTS IN THE PARLOR, FIRE IN THE GRATE
                                D   G
    CLOCK ON THE MANTLE SAYING IT'S GETTING LATE

    CURTAINS ON THE WINDOW SNOWY WHITE
                         D   G
    THE PARLOR IS PLEASANT ON SUNDAY NIGHT

        G
        IDA RED, IDA RED
                        D   G
        I'M PLUMB FOOL ABOUT IDA RED

    G
2. LAMP ON THE TABLE, A PICTURE ON THE WALL
                           D   G
    THERE'S A PRETTY SOFA AND THAT'S NOT ALL

    I'M NOT MISTAKEN I'M SURE I'M RIGHT
                                D   G
    THERE'S SOMEBODY ELSE IN THE PARLOR TONIGHT

        CHORUS

    G
3. CHICKEN IN THE BREAD TRAY PECKIN' OUT DOUGH
                              D   G
    GRANNY DOES YOUR DOG BITE NO CHILD NO

    HURRY UP BOYS AND DON'T FOOL AROUND
                            D   G
    GRAB YOUR PARTNER, TRUCK ON DOWN

        CHORUS

    G
4. LIGHTS ARE BURNING DIM, THE FIRES ARE GETTING LOW
                             D   G
    SOMEBODY SAYS IT'S TIME TO GO

    I HEAR THE WHISPER GENTLE AND LIGHT
                             D   G
    DON'T FORGET TO COME NEXT SUNDAY NIGHT

        CHORUS

SWITCHING BETWEEN G AND A

In 1927 Dock Boggs recorded a tune he called "Country Blues" with an Appalachian clawhammer banjo accompaniment, a performance that was included on the landmark *Anthology of American Folk Music,* edited by Harry Smith. It has since been recorded countless times, often under the name "Darling Corey." On the following page is a simple version using two chords, A and G, that will give you plenty of practice switching between those two chords. Use a strum with upstrokes on the second and fourth beats:

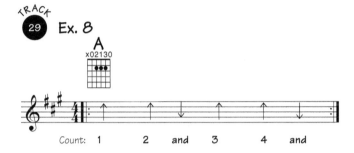

PRACTICE TIPS

If the switches are a little rough, go through the same process we went through with G and D. First just try to make it from an A chord to the low note of the G chord (Example 9). Then go from A to two notes of the G chord (Example 10). And finally just loop a couple of measures, going back and forth between A and G (Example 11).

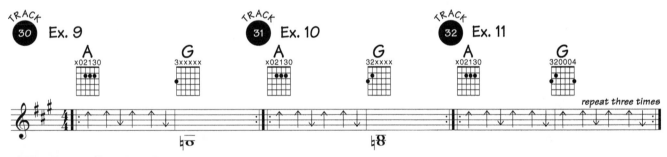

ESSENTIAL LISTENING

Harry Smith assembled the landmark ***Anthology of American Folk Music*** for the Folkways label in 1952. Today, when so much material by prewar folk artists is routinely reassembled, remastered, and reissued in indestructible digital clarity, it's hard to understand the impact Smith's six-LP set had on the emerging folk-revival population. Recordings by Blind Lemon Jefferson, Frank Hutchison, Dock Boggs, and Sleepy John Estes had been commercially unavailable for decades; the *Anthology* put their music in the hands of young musicians like Dave Van Ronk, Jerry Garcia, David Bromberg, John Fahey, and Bob Dylan, who interpreted, performed, recorded, and sometimes rewrote many *Anthology* songs for a new generation in the 1960s.

Dock Boggs' "Country Blues," featured on the *Anthology,* was recently covered by slide guitarist Kelly Joe Phelps on *Shine Eyed Mister Zen* (Rykodisc). Recordings of the tune as **"Darling Corey"** include *Weavers at Carnegie Hall* (Vanguard) and the Seldom Scene's *Act One* (Rebel).

DARLING COREY

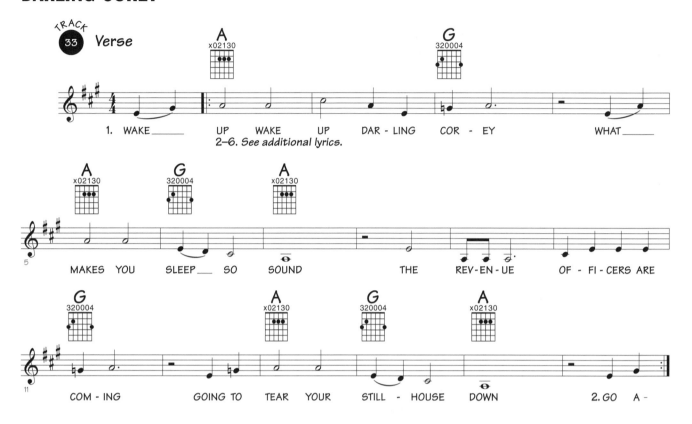

1. WAKE___ UP WAKE UP DAR-LING COR-EY WHAT___
   2–6. *See additional lyrics.*

MAKES YOU SLEEP___ SO SOUND   THE REV-EN-UE OF-FI-CERS ARE

COM-ING   GOING TO TEAR YOUR STILL-HOUSE DOWN   2. GO A-

<table>
<tr><td>

      A   G

1. WAKE UP, WAKE UP DARLING COREY
     A   G   A
WHAT MAKES YOU SLEEP SO SOUND
            G
THE REVENUE OFFICERS ARE COMING
     A   G   A
GOING TO TEAR YOUR STILLHOUSE DOWN

      A   G

2. GO AWAY, GO AWAY DARLING COREY
     A   G   A
QUIT HANGING AROUND MY BED
            G
BAD LIQUOR HAS RUINED MY BODY
     A   G   A
PRETTY WOMEN HAVE GONE TO MY HEAD

      A   G

3. DIG A HOLE, DIG A HOLE IN THE MEADOW
     A   G   A
DIG A HOLE IN THE COLD, COLD GROUND
            G
DIG A HOLE, DIG A HOLE IN THE MEADOW
     A   G   A
GOING TO LAY DARLING COREY DOWN

</td><td>

      A   G

4. THE LAST TIME I SEEN DARLING COREY
     A   G   A
ON THE BANKS OF THE DEEP BLUE SEA
            G
SHE HAD A FORTY-FOUR BUCKLED AROUND HER
     A   G   A
AND A BANJO ON HER KNEE

      A   G

5. DIG A HOLE, DIG A HOLE IN THE MEADOW
     A   G   A
DIG A HOLE IN THE COLD, COLD GROUND
            G
DIG A HOLE, DIG A HOLE IN THE MEADOW
     A   G   A
GOING TO LAY DARLING COREY DOWN

      A   G

6. CAN'T YOU HEAR THEM BLUEBIRDS A-SINGIN'
     A   G   A
DON'T YOU HEAR THAT MOURNFUL SOUND?
            G
THEY'RE PREACHING DARLING COREY'S FUNERAL
     A   G   A
IN SOME LONESOME GRAVEYARD GROUND

</td></tr>
</table>

LESSON 6
THE C CHORD

Here is the fingering for C. Notice that your ring and middle fingers are doing what they do on a G chord, only up a string. To practice switching from G to C, first see if you can move your middle and ring fingers together, from the sixth and fifth strings to the fifth and fourth strings:

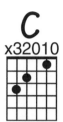

Once you can make that move, you can start working in your pinky on the G and your index finger on the C to switch between the complete chords.

PLAY IT

Playing on a two-chord tune will also help you get in the groove of switching between G and C. "Hot Corn, Cold Corn" is basically about making moonshine (moonshine being a kind of corn liquor and a demijohn a kind of jug to hold it). Use this strum pattern:

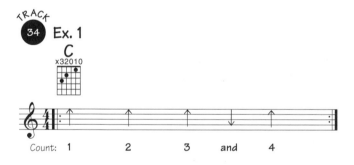

TRACK 34 Ex. 1

Count: 1   2   3   and   4

ESSENTIAL LISTENING

Banjoist **Earl Scruggs** and guitarist/singer **Lester Flatt** were the first of many bluegrass greats to graduate from Bill Monroe's Blue Grass Boys, departing to form Flatt and Scruggs and the Foggy Mountain Boys in the late 1940s. Well received on the bluegrass circuit, Flatt and Scruggs were subsequently embraced by the folk revival crowd, in large part because of Scruggs' brilliant three-finger picking style. While Flatt generally played rhythm and sang, he goes down in guitar history for popularizing the "G-run," a bass-string figure used to fill out out a phrase on the way into a break or the next vocal line.

Their performance of **"Hot Corn, Cold Corn"** can be heard on *Flatt and Scruggs at Carnegie Hall: The Complete Concert* (Koch). You can also hear the song on the Holy Modal Rounders' collection *1 & 2* (Fantasy) and on Jerry Garcia and David Grisman's *Not for Kids Only* (Acoustic Disc).

Notice the extra two beats of G near the end and the fact that there are two more bars of C after that, the whole thing adding up to a somewhat untidy 10½ bars. So far every tune we've done has fit into a neater, more typical eight-bar shape. What's going on?

Well, this happens a good deal in country and blues: the accompaniment is tailored around the vocal, and if the singer phrases in a way that drags out the line for effect (in this case, the "yes, sir"), the chords are stretched out underneath to accommodate that—in this case, holding on to the G for two extra beats. Once you're back on the C chord, there's a little breathing room provided (literally, for the singer) before kicking off the next verse.

HOT CORN, COLD CORN

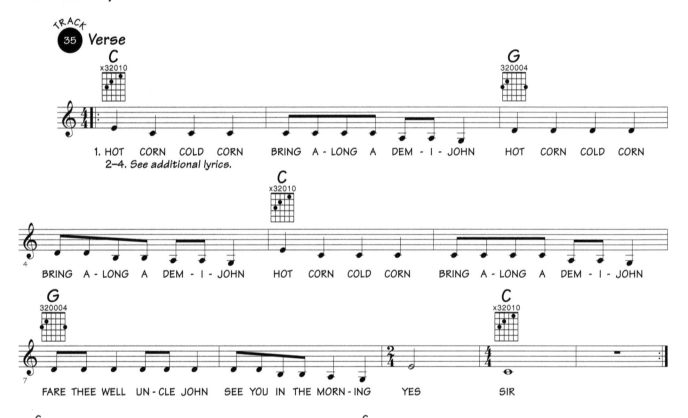

1. HOT CORN, COLD CORN, BRING ALONG A DEMIJOHN
   G
   HOT CORN, COLD CORN, BRING ALONG A DEMIJOHN
   C
   HOT CORN, COLD CORN, BRING ALONG A DEMIJOHN
   G
   FARE THEE WELL, UNCLE JOHN, SEE YOU IN THE MORNING
      C
   YES, SIR

2. *C*
   UPSTAIRS, DOWNSTAIRS, OUT IN THE KITCHEN
   G
   UPSTAIRS, DOWNSTAIRS, OUT IN THE KITCHEN
   C
   UPSTAIRS, DOWNSTAIRS, OUT IN THE KITCHEN
   G
   SEE UNCLE BILL, HE'S A RARIN' AND A PITCHIN'
      C
   YES, SIR

3. *C*
   OLD AUNT PEGGY WON'T YOU FILL 'EM UP AGAIN
   G
   OLD AUNT PEGGY WON'T YOU FILL 'EM UP AGAIN
   C
   OLD AUNT PEGGY WON'T YOU FILL 'EM UP AGAIN
   G
   AIN'T HAD A DRINK SINCE I DON'T KNOW WHEN
      C
   YES, SIR

4. *C*
   YONDER COME THE PREACHER AND THE CHILDREN ARE A-CRYIN'
   G
   YONDER COME THE PREACHER AND THE CHILDREN ARE A-CRYIN'
   C
   YONDER COME THE PREACHER AND THE CHILDREN ARE A-CRYIN'
   G
   CHICKENS ARE A-HOLLERIN', TOENAILS A-FLYIN'
      C
   YES, SIR

LESSON 7
MORE SINGLE NOTES

Time for a little more melody playing. Let's add in two more notes on the second string, C and D. C is played at the first fret on the second string and notated in the second space from the top of the staff. D is played at the third fret of the second string and notated on the second line from the top of the staff.

Playing the next two examples will help you get used to finding these new notes. Example 1 is just notes on the second string; in Example 2, you're combining those notes with ones you already know on the third string.

TRACK 36 Ex. 1

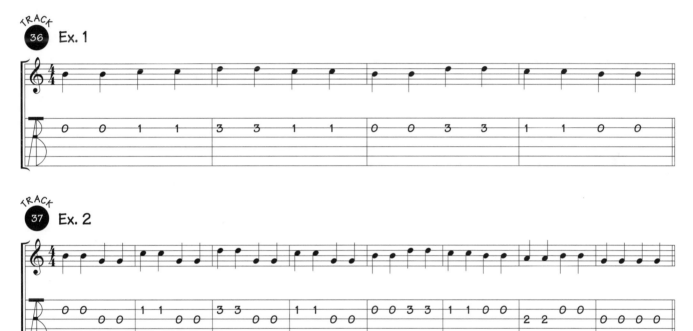

TRACK 37 Ex. 2

BACK TO "SALLY"

Now we turn to the second section of the fiddle tune "Sally Goodin," as advertised a few pages back. There are eighth notes again, just as there are in the first section. Take it slowly, using downstrokes and upstrokes as marked. Once you've got the second section down, try putting the whole thing together.

You'll notice that in the full rendition of the song, chords are shown up above the melody. On the CD, you will hear an accompaniment part in the left channel; the melody is in the right. You now know enough chords and single notes to try both parts. Pan your stereo right or left if you want to isolate either the lead or the accompaniment. The accompaniment part uses the strum in Example 3.

TRACK 38 Ex. 3

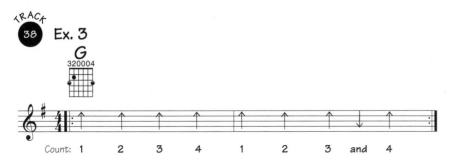

SALLY GOODIN

LESSON 8
COUNTRY BACKUP BASICS

So far we've been doing strum patterns where we always brush across all the strings of a chord with the pick using various combinations of upstrokes and downstrokes. Now we're going to learn our first country backup pattern, in which we'll combine strumming full chords with picking out individual bass notes. This approach is also referred to as bluegrass rhythm or simply a "boom-chick" pattern.

So here it is, our first bass/strum move. It's not so different from doing four straight downstroke strums, except that the first strum is replaced with a single note, the *root* of the chord. The root of a C chord is the note C. We've learned the C on the second string; there's another C on the guitar at the third fret of the fifth string. We've actually already fretted this note, as part of playing a C chord. It is notated on the first ledger line below the staff. Those two C notes are an octave apart. If you play or sing them, you'll hear that they are in tune with each other.

To do a bass note and strum together, play a single low C on the first beat, followed by three strums on beats 2, 3, and 4 (Example 1).

Got all that? There's more, if you want to do the same kind of move on a G chord. There's a G an octave down from the open third string, and it's played at the third fret of the sixth string. We've already been fretting and playing this note as part of a G chord. At right you can see how the low G is notated. In Example 2, try using it in a G-chord bass/strum: play the low G on the first beat, followed by three strums. Then, in Example 3, try switching between a C chord and a G chord.

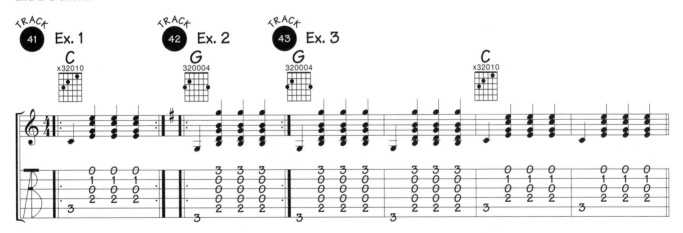

The root of a D chord is D, or the open fourth string, which you've already played in "Sally Goodin." For a D-chord bass/strum, play D for the bass note, then strum the top three strings, as in Example 4 on the next page. In Example 5, try switching between G and D.

When you come back to the G, as long as you get your ring finger down on the low string in time for the bass note on beat 1, you've actually got an extra beat in which to get the rest of your hand in place. Take advantage of this extra breathing room.

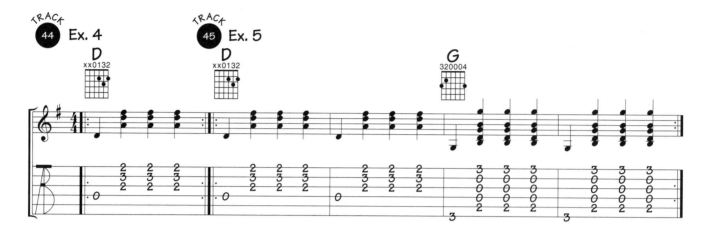

Let's play a song from the folk and bluegrass repertoire in the key of G with our bass/strum pattern.

EAST VIRGINIA BLUES

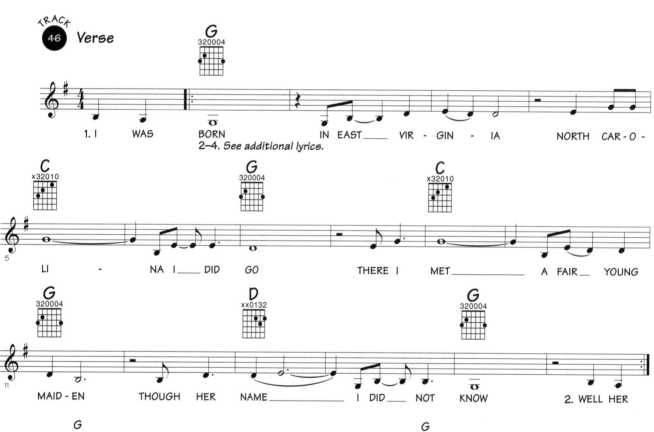

1. I WAS BORN IN EAST VIRGINIA
   $\quad\quad\quad\quad$ C $\quad\quad$ G
   NORTH CAROLINA I DID GO
   $\quad\quad$ C $\quad\quad\quad\quad\quad$ G
   THERE I MET A FAIR YOUNG MAIDEN
   $\quad\quad\quad\quad\quad$ D $\quad\quad\quad$ G
   THOUGH HER NAME I DID NOT KNOW

2. WELL HER HAIR WAS DARK IN COLOR
   $\quad\quad$ C $\quad\quad\quad\quad$ G
   AND HER CHEEKS WERE ROSY RED
   $\quad\quad$ C $\quad\quad\quad\quad\quad$ G
   ON HER BREAST SHE WORE WHITE LILIES
   $\quad\quad\quad$ D $\quad\quad\quad\quad$ G
   WHERE I LONGED TO LAY MY HEAD

3. I DON'T WANT YOUR GREENBACK DOLLAR
   $\quad\quad\quad\quad$ C $\quad\quad\quad\quad$ G
   I DON'T WANT YOUR SILVER CHAIN
   $\quad\quad\quad\quad$ C $\quad\quad\quad\quad\quad$ G
   ALL I WANT IS YOUR HEART, DARLING
   $\quad\quad\quad\quad\quad$ D $\quad\quad\quad$ G
   WON'T YOU TAKE ME BACK AGAIN

4. I'D RATHER BE IN SOME DARK HOLLER
   $\quad\quad\quad\quad$ C $\quad\quad\quad\quad$ G
   WHERE THE SUN REFUSE TO SHINE
   $\quad\quad\quad\quad\quad\quad$ C $\quad\quad\quad$ G
   THAN FOR YOU TO BE ANOTHER'S DARLING
   $\quad\quad\quad\quad$ D $\quad\quad\quad\quad$ G
   AND TO KNOW YOU'LL NEVER BE MINE

LESSON 9
SEVENTH CHORDS

The G7 chord, as you might guess, is closely related to G. Two of the three fingers for this chord are the same as for G—only the high string changes, from the third fret with your pinky to the first fret with your index finger.

The G7 feels and looks a little like a wider, more spread-out C chord. You can use the same trick of first switching just your middle and ring fingers between G7 and C before switching between the full three-finger version of each chord. Then spend a little time switching between C and G7 just using a basic strum, as in Example 1.

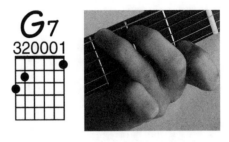

G7
320001

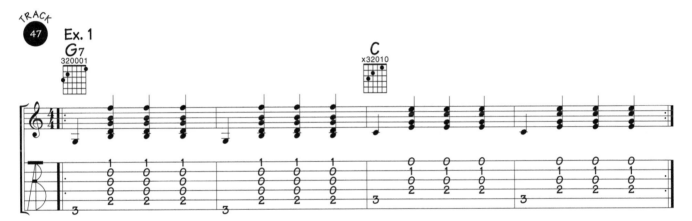

TRACK 47 **Ex. 1**

G7 320001   **C** x32010

It's a good idea to be able to switch between G and G7 as well. In Example 2, practice getting your pinky out of the way and getting your index finger in there on the first fret.

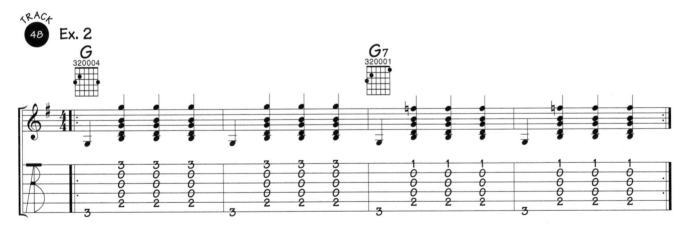

TRACK 48 **Ex. 2**

G 320004   **G7** 320001

D7 is closely related to D. When you look at the diagram, you can see that the two chords differ by only one note: on a D7, you play the first fret on the second string rather than the third fret, as on a regular D. But unlike switching from G to G7, going from a D to a D7 means switching to a whole new chord shape.

The D7 also creates a whole new sound. Seventh chords have a tangier sound often associated with the blues, and they help strengthen the transition between certain chords—in this case, changing the D to D7 strengthens the return to G. Listen for this while you try a few switches between a standard G chord and a D7 with a basic strum (Example 3).

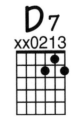

D7
xx0213

TRACK 49 Ex. 3

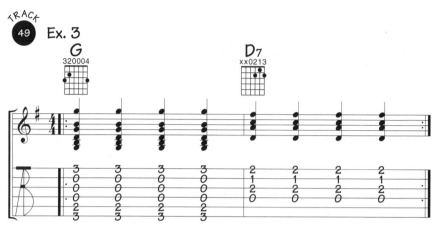

Now try it using the bass/strum we just learned:

TRACK 50 Ex. 4

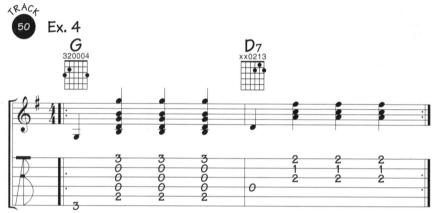

ESSENTIAL LISTENING

Buell Kazee's rendition of **"East Virginia Blues"** can be heard on Harry Smith's *Anthology of American Folk Music* (Smithsonian Folkways). A 1934 recording by **the Carter Family**, featuring pioneering country guitarist Maybelle Carter, can be heard on *Longing for Old Virginia: Their Complete Victor Recordings, 1934* (Rounder). John Duffy and the Country Gentlemen recorded a bluegrass version on *Live in Japan* (Rebel), and more recently Dave Alvin's *Public Domain* (HighTone) included a revved-up version with twangin', slapback-echoed guitars.

BACK TO "VIRGINIA"

We can work both G7 and D7 into "East Virginia Blues." The bass/strum pattern remains exactly the same, but there's a G7 slipped into measures 3 and 4 and a D7 in measures 13 and 14. Listen for how the G7 strengthens the switch from G up to C.

EAST VIRGINIA BLUES

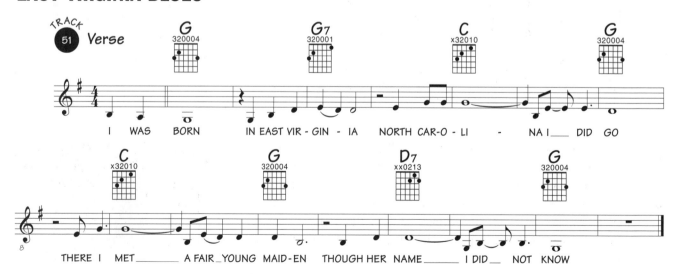

LESSON 10
WALTZ TIME

All the songs we've played so far have been in 4/4 time. That is, we've been using quarter notes as our basic unit to count with, and we've been counting out four quarter notes per measure. The symbol 4/4 at the beginning of the staff actually means:

$\frac{4}{4}$ ← Four beats per measure
← Quarter note (4) gets one beat

In waltz or 3/4 time, you still count in quarter notes, but there are only three of them in a bar. I know, I know, how can you have only three-quarters of some-thing? It doesn't seem to make sense. But this is the way it is. The 3/4 symbol means:

$\frac{3}{4}$ ← Three beats per measure
← Quarter note (4) gets one beat

If we take our brand-new bass/strum pattern in 4/4 and lop off the last beat, we'll have a strum that works in 3/4. Here are the strums for G, C, and D.

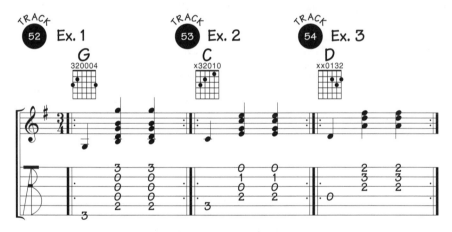

Now we're playing only three beats for each measure. You don't have quite as much time to switch chords now, because you have one fewer beat in each mea-sure, so it really helps if you get on that one bass note of the chord right away and get your other fingers there in time for the strums on beats 2 and 3. Of course, if you're going to a D, D7, A, or E chord, your bass note is an open string, which gives you that much more time to form the rest of the chord.

PLAY IT

The bluesy bluegrass tune "In the Pines" is in 3/4 and gives you another chance to take those new G7 and D7 chords out for a spin.

ESSENTIAL LISTENING

In christening his band the Blue Grass Boys, after his home state of Kentucky, mandolinist and singer **Bill Monroe** gave the world a name for the genre that he arguably invented single-handedly. Monroe got his start as a professional with his older brother Charlie, and by 1939 he had struck out on his own, landing a job on the Grand Ole Opry. Over the next decade Monroe assembled the first definitive bluegrass ensemble and transformed the old-time string band music and songs he had grown up with into a technically demanding, vocally exhilarating art form.

"In the Pines" was in Monroe's repertoire from early on; one performance can be heard on *The Father of Bluegrass: The Early Years: 1940–1947* (ASV/Living Era). Other versions can be heard on *When I Stop Dreaming: Best of the Louvin Brothers* (Razor and Tie), Dave Van Ronk's *Folkways Years: 1959–1961* (Smithsonian Folkways), and Todd Phillips' tribute to Bill Monroe, *In the Pines* (Gourd).

IN THE PINES

1.
```
        G        G7    C    G
   THE LONGEST TRAIN I EVER SAW
              D7        G
   WENT DOWN THAT GEORGIA LINE
            G7       C    G
   THE ENGINE PASSED AT SIX O'CLOCK
              D7     G
   AND THE CAB PASSED BY AT NINE

                   G7
   IN THE PINES, IN THE PINES
              C         G
   WHERE THE SUN NEVER SHINES
                     D7          G
   AND WE SHIVERED WHEN THE COLD WINDS BLOW
```

2.
```
      G      G7         C    G
   I ASKED MY CAPTAIN FOR THE TIME OF DAY
                   D7      G
   HE SAID HE THROWED HIS WATCH AWAY
               G7      C        G
   IT'S A LONG STEEL RAIL AND A SHORT CROSS-TIE
            D7     G
   I'M ON MY WAY BACK HOME
```

CHORUS

3.
```
         G           G7       C    G
   LITTLE GIRL, LITTLE GIRL, WHAT HAVE I DONE
                 D7        G
   THAT MAKES YOU TREAT ME SO
                   G7       C          G
   YOU'VE CAUSED ME TO WEEP, YOU'VE CAUSED ME TO MOAN
                    D7      G
   YOU'VE CAUSED ME TO LEAVE MY HOME
```

CHORUS

LESSON 11
HALF NOTES AND RESTS

The melodies we have played so far have used only quarter and eighth notes, and now it is time to introduce a little more variety. Let's start with the *half note* (♩), which we talked about in our earlier discussion of rhythm basics but haven't used yet. Just like half a dollar is twice as much as a quarter dollar, a half note lasts twice as long as a quarter note. Since a quarter note gets one beat, it stands to reason that the half note gets two. So in Example 1, you pick the string only on beats 1 and 3 in each measure. To really see and hear the difference between quarter and half notes, try switching between them while counting as in Example 2.

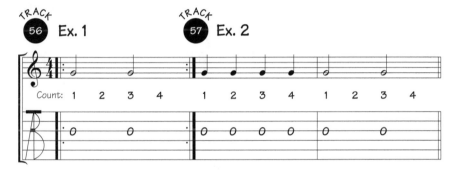

THE REST OF THE STORY

Sometimes a melody also calls for not playing *anything* at a certain point. Instead of a note, you have a *rest,* during which you stop playing while the count goes on. There are quarter-note rests (𝄽), where you don't play for one beat, as well as half-note rests (▬), where you don't play for two beats.

Try Example 3, which includes half-note rests. A quarter-note rest means you don't play for just one beat, while you keep counting. Try Example 4, in which you rest on the first beat of each measure.

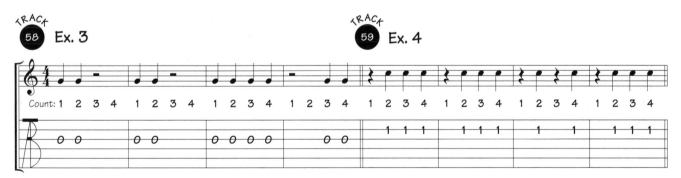

BANKS OF THE OHIO

The murder ballad "Banks of the Ohio" was in the repertoire of both the Carter Family and the Monroe Brothers (the duo of Bill Monroe and his brother James). This version of the melody uses half notes and quarter notes. Notice that the melody does not begin on the first beat of a measure but on the second beat. In Example 5 start counting beforehand, and pick the first note the second time you hit beat 2. Many of the phrases within the tune also start on the second beat, after a quarter-note rest.

Once again, the accompaniment chords are included above the melody and recorded on the CD on the left channel. The accompaniment part uses the strum in Example 6.

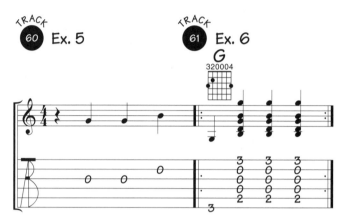

BANKS OF THE OHIO

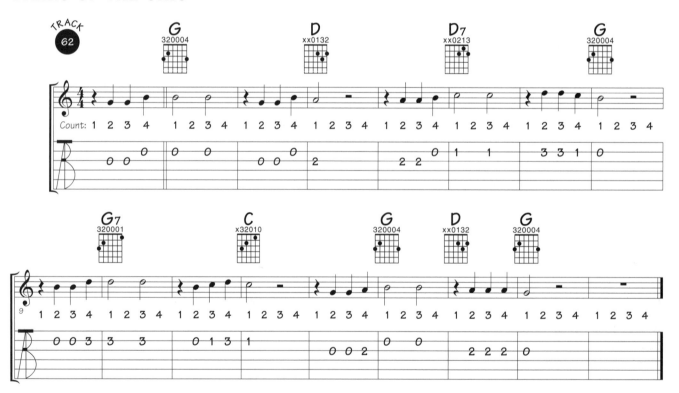

ESSENTIAL LISTENING

A good number of American ballads are the descendants of songs from the British Isles, some of them hundreds of years old, many of them with countless verses and variations. Many **murder ballads,** which are numerous enough to qualify as a subcategory, have a distinctly American flavor. "Tom Dooley," for example, which was handed down over several generations in North Carolina, tells the apparently true story of a local 19th-century crime and hanging. "Banks of the Ohio" tells the classic murder ballad story, as do "Pretty Polly" and "Omie Wise" (and, without the murder itself, "Careless Love"): boy meets girl, boy courts girl, boy deceives girl, boy murders girl.

An often-played song, **"Banks of the Ohio"** can be heard on recordings by Doc Watson (*On Stage,* Vanguard), Joan Baez (*Volume 2,* Vanguard), Ralph Stanley (*Saturday Night and Sunday Morning,* Freeland), and Tony Rice (*Tony Rice,* Rounder), among many others.

LESSON 12
MINOR CHORDS

So far we've been playing all *major* chords, which are characterized by a straightforward, happy sound. But maybe all those bright 'n' chirpy sounds are starting to get to you. Even if all the lyrics *are* about death and hard times, you want something to suit your brooding, mysterious personality. When, I hear you ask, are we going to get to the really dark stuff? Right now: here are our first two *minor* chords, E minor and A minor:

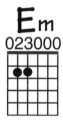

E minor is like an *easier* version of E: start with an E chord, then lift your index finger. Done! That's E minor.

A minor is also straightforward: take a regular E chord and just move the whole thing, all three fingers, up one string, keeping everything else exactly the same.

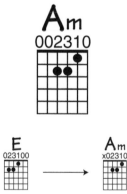

BASS AND STRUM

Play an open E on the low sixth string to start the bass/strum pattern for an E-minor chord, and play an open A on the fifth string to start the bass/strum pattern on an A minor. The note E is shown in the space three ledger lines below the staff, and the note A is shown on the second ledger line below the staff. Try doing a bass/strum pattern on each of these two chords.

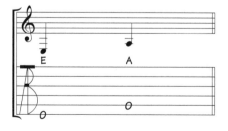

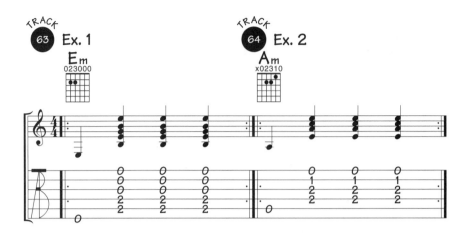

ARE YOU GOING . . .

"Scarborough Fair" has been around for centuries, but it was popularized in the 1960s by Paul Simon's arrangement of it for Simon and Garfunkel. Even without all their tricky layers of guitar parts, it's a challenging tune, as it involves several chords and you never stay on one chord for long. As a song for learning to switch between minor and major chords, it can't be beat, and of course it is a beautiful song. So here it is. It's in 3/4, so take the above bass/strum patterns on E and A minor and lop off the fourth beat.

SCARBOROUGH FAIR

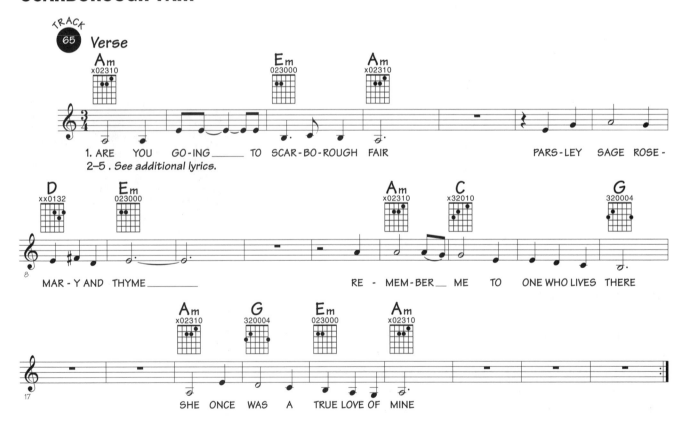

	Am		Em	Am
1.	ARE YOU GOING TO SCARBOROUGH FAIR			
			D	Em
	PARSLEY, SAGE, ROSEMARY, AND THYME			
	Am	C		G
	REMEMBER ME TO ONE WHO LIVES THERE			
	Am	G	Em	Am
	SHE ONCE WAS A TRUE LOVE OF MINE			

	Am		Em	Am
2.	TELL HER TO MAKE ME A CAMBRIC SHIRT			
			D	Em
	PARSLEY, SAGE, ROSEMARY, AND THYME			
	Am	C		G
	WITHOUT ANY SEAM OR NEEDLEWORK			
	Am	G	Em	Am
	THEN SHE'LL BE A TRUE LOVE OF MINE			

```
      Am                    Em    Am
3.    TELL HER TO FIND ME AN ACRE OF LAND
                            D       Em
      PARSLEY, SAGE, ROSEMARY, AND THYME
        Am          C              G
      BETWEEN THE SALT WATER AND THE SEA STRAND
      Am        G   Em           Am
      THEN SHE'LL BE A TRUE LOVE OF MINE
```

```
      Am                    Em    Am
4.    PLOW THE LAND WITH THE HORN OF A LAMB
                            D       Em
      PARSLEY, SAGE, ROSEMARY, AND THYME
        Am          C                      G
      THEN SOW SOME SEEDS FROM NORTH OF THE DAM
      Am        G   Em           Am
      THEN SHE'LL BE A TRUE LOVE OF MINE
```

```
      Am                    Em    Am
5.    TELL HER TO REAP IT WITH A SICKLE OF LEATHER
                            D       Em
      PARSLEY, SAGE, ROSEMARY, AND THYME
        Am          C              G
      AND GATHER IT ALL IN A BUNCH OF HEATHER
      Am        G   Em           Am
      THEN SHE'LL BE A TRUE LOVE OF MINE
```

ESSENTIAL LISTENING

Nowadays we use the terms *folksinger* and *singer-songwriter* interchangeably, but until the mid-1960s a folksinger meant someone interested in folk songs—that is, in collecting, learning, and performing a repertoire of traditional music. The songs themselves, along with their origins and genealogies, were of particular interest. In Britain, prior to his associations with Fairport Convention and Steeleye Span, **Martin Carthy** was known as an especially thorough researcher who brought many traditional tunes to light.

In 1965, Carthy's rendition of **"Scarborough Fair"** caught the ear of a visiting American named Paul Simon, who popularized the tune beyond all imagination. Check out Carthy's version on his debut album from 1965 (*Martin Carthy*, Topic), or listen to Simon and Garfunkel's pop classic on *Parsley, Sage, Rosemary, and Thyme* (Columbia), with its crystalline acoustic guitar arpeggios and canonlike vocal arrangement.

LESSON 13
A MINOR-KEY MELODY

Now that we have learned some minor chords, let's play a melody in a minor key.

"Shady Grove" is a great folk song in a minor key. Measures 6 and 7 of this tune include a few string crossings where it can be tricky to keep your picking hand alternating evenly between downstrokes and upstrokes. It's often a good practice idea to isolate the most challenging parts of a tune and work on them separately, as in Examples 1 and 2, as well as playing the whole tune through.

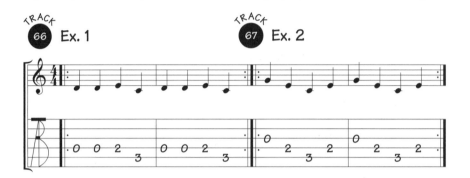

This arrangement includes one new note on the fingerboard, F, which is played at the third fret of the fourth string. It's shown in the first space on the staff.

For now, we will play the melody without any accompaniment.

SHADY GROVE

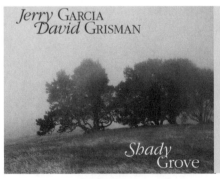

ESSENTIAL LISTENING

You can hear Bill Monroe doing **"Shady Grove"** with Peter Rowan and Tex Logan on the sprawling *Folk Music at Newport*, Vol. 1 (Vanguard). The New Lost City Ramblers include the tune on their reunion CD *There Ain't No Way Out* (Smithsonian Folkways), and the alt-country Blood Oranges did it on their debut, *Corn River* (East Side Digital). "Shady Grove" has also been the title cut of both a 1969 Quicksilver Messenger Service LP (reissued on One Way) and a collection of traditional songs and instrumentals by Grateful Dead guitarist Jerry Garcia and mandolinist David Grisman (Acoustic Disc).

LESSON 14
THE B7 CHORD

B7 is our first chord so far to require all four of your fretting fingers. The three lowest notes are actually fingered just like a D7 chord but on different strings, which is one way to get your fingers into this shape a little quicker. Try getting your index, middle, and ring fingers into place before worrying about your pinky.

SWITCHING BETWEEN B7 AND E

When you switch between B7 and E, your middle finger can stay planted right there on the second fret of the fifth string for both chords. Your index and ring fingers trade strings, and they don't even have to go to different frets. Just move your index finger from the first fret, fourth string, to the first fret, third string. And move your ring finger from the second fret, third string, to the second fret, fourth string. Then bring in your pinky on the second fret of the high string. Try it.

TRACK **69** Ex. 1

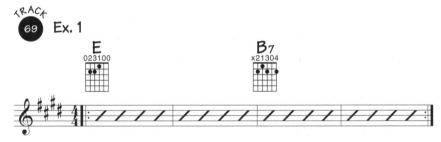

SWITCHING BETWEEN B7 AND A

Your fingers stay in the same order across the strings whether you're playing a B7 or an A. To get to an A from B7, lift up all four of your fingers and move the middle, index, and ring fingers over one string. When you get there, bring your index finger up one fret so it's on the second fret along with your other two fingers. Your pinky gets to take a rest on the A.

Going from A to B7, try moving your three fingers from the A chord into place for the bottom of the B7 chord, *then* worry about getting your pinky into place on the first string.

TRACK **70** Ex. 2

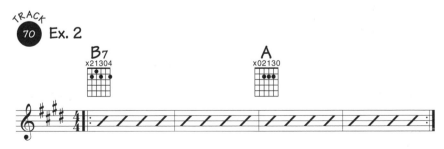

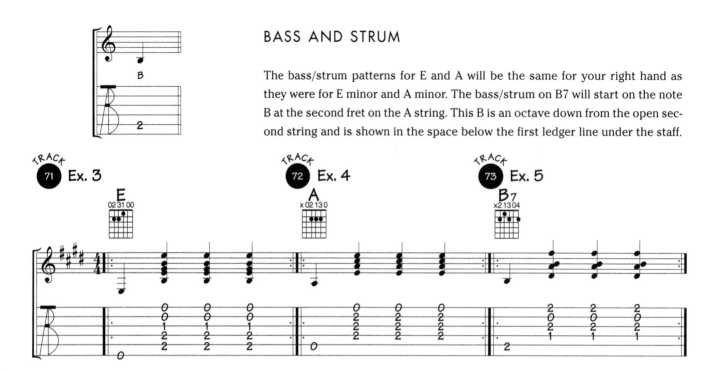

BASS AND STRUM

The bass/strum patterns for E and A will be the same for your right hand as they were for E minor and A minor. The bass/strum on B7 will start on the note B at the second fret on the A string. This B is an octave down from the open second string and is shown in the space below the first ledger line under the staff.

O BROTHER

"Man of Constant Sorrow," an old song that was introduced to the bluegrass world by the Stanley Brothers, gained a certain notoriety as the theme song of the Soggy Bottom Boys in the Coen Brothers' film *O Brother, Where Art Thou?* (where it was actually sung by Dan Tyminski, a multi-instrumentalist who plays in the band of bluegrass bandleader/fiddler Alison Krauss). We'll play it in E using our bass/strum pattern, and there will be plenty of switches between B7 and A and between B7 and E.

MAN OF CONSTANT SORROW

RAISED

E	A
1.	I AM A MAN OF CONSTANT SORROW

E   **A**
1. I AM A MAN OF CONSTANT SORROW
    B7   **E**
  I'VE SEEN TROUBLE ALL MY DAYS
          A
  I LEFT MY HOME IN OLD KENTUCKY
       B7   **E** **B7 E**
  THE STATE WHERE I WAS BORN AND RAISED

E   **A**
2. FOR SIX LONG YEARS I'VE BEEN IN TROUBLE
    B7   **E**
  NO PLEASURE HERE ON EARTH I FIND
          A
  FOR IN THIS WORLD I'M BOUND TO RAMBLE
    B7   **E** **B7 E**
  I HAVE NO FRIENDS TO HELP ME NOW

E   **A**
3. YOU CAN BURY ME IN SOME DEEP VALLEY
    B7   **E**
  FOR MANY YEARS WHERE I MAY LAY
          A
  THEN YOU MAY LEARN TO LOVE ANOTHER
     B7   **E** **B7 E**
  WHILE I AM SLEEPING IN MY GRAVE

E   **A**
4. MAYBE YOUR FRIENDS THINK I'M JUST A STRANGER
    B7   **E**
  MY FACE YOU NEVER WILL SEE NO MORE
          A
  BUT THERE IS ONE PROMISE THAT IS GIVEN
    B7   **E** **B7 E**
  I'LL MEET YOU ON GOD'S GOLDEN SHORE

ESSENTIAL LISTENING

The **Stanley Brothers** (Ralph Stanley on banjo and tenor vocal, Carter Stanley on guitar and lead vocal) became one of the first bluegrass groups to succeed in the wake of Bill Monroe's string band revolution of the 1940s. Carter Stanley passed away at the early age of 41, but Ralph continued on with his band, the Clinch Mountain Boys, performing classic instrumentals such as "Clinch Mountain Backstep" and old mountain songs, including **"Man of Constant Sorrow"** (check out any of their versions, including the one on *The Best of the Best of the Stanley Brothers,* Federal). You can hear music by Ralph Stanley and the Stanley Brothers on the soundtrack to *O Brother, Where Art Thou?* (Mercury), which included several other artists' versions of "Constant Sorrow" as well. Also of note: the version on *Bob Dylan* (Columbia).

CONGRATULATIONS

You've made it through Book 1! You now know almost a dozen chords and several ways to strum them, most of the notes of the fingerboard in first position, and plenty of new songs. Whether you keep working on the material here for a little while or plunge right into Book 2, here are two suggestions. First, try to chase down a few of the recommended recordings. It's important to hear what the artists we've been talking about really sounded like, so you can form your own opinions and tastes. This great roots music is bound to inspire you. And second, it's called playing music, so don't forget to just play. Not because you have to, not because you haven't been practicing—just because you feel like it and it's fun.

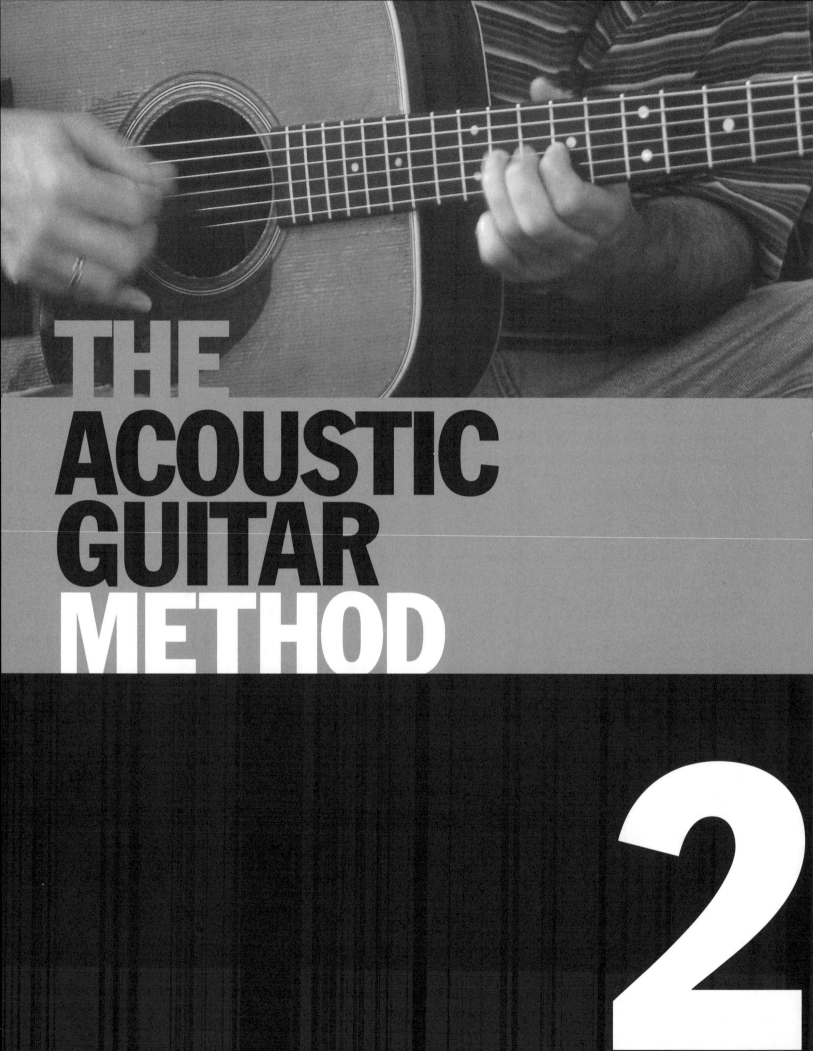

THE
ACOUSTIC
GUITAR
METHOD

2

WELCOME

Introduction

Tune-Up

Greetings, guitarist. Yes, as an esteemed graduate of Book 1, you are a guitarist now, playing real music: you know a variety of open chords and strums, some single-note melodies, and almost a dozen songs. Check out the summary of Book 1 below, pat yourself on the back for learning all that stuff already (see the Music Notation Key if you need a little refresher on how to read the music), and then get ready to dig in deeper.

In Book 2, you'll learn how to alternate the bass notes in a country backup pattern, how to connect chords with some classic bass runs, and how to play your first fingerpicking patterns. As you learn to play more tunes, you'll find out what makes a major scale work and what blue notes do to a melody, all while learning more notes on the fingerboard. And, of course, along the way you'll be learning to play more great songs from the American roots repertoire.

WHAT WE LEARNED IN BOOK 1

Chords

Notes

Strums

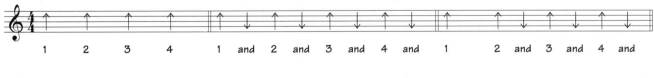

LESSON 1
THE ALTERNATING BASS

In Book 1, we played country backup parts by hitting a bass note on the first beat and following up with three downstroke strums (or two downstroke strums for a waltz). Now we're going to add in another bass note, on the third beat, replacing one of the strums and giving us the classic country and blue-grass sound of an *alternating bass.*

Let's start with a familiar chord, D. For now, our general rule is: for the second bass note of the pattern, go up to the next highest string (meaning the string with the next highest *pitch,* not the one higher off the floor). So for a D chord, we'll play the second fret, third string, on beat 3, as in Example 1. Everything is still done with all downstrokes (toward the floor).

On an A chord, if we follow the general rule of going up to the next highest string for the bass note, we'll play an E note, or the second fret on the fourth string, on beat 3. It will sound like Example 2. You're now playing a bass note on every other beat, and following every bass note with a downward strum on the top strings.

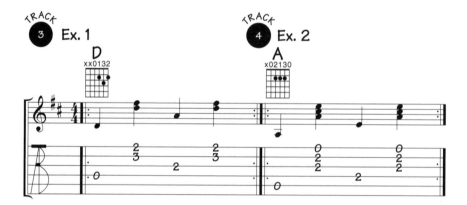

As you might have guessed, the interesting part is keeping this going as you switch chords. To get used to maintaining an alternating-bass strum for each chord, practice switching between D and A every two bars, as in Example 3.

If you're having trouble hitting the right strings for the bass notes, take out the strums for a moment. Just try socking away at the first and third beats of the D chord, as in Example 4, paying attention to hitting each string as accurately as possible. You should still finger the whole chord while you do this exercise. In Example 5, do the same thing with the A chord: just play the bass notes.

When you go back to playing the whole strum, continue to focus on hitting the bass notes on beats 1 and 3, and let the strums fall almost as an afterthought.

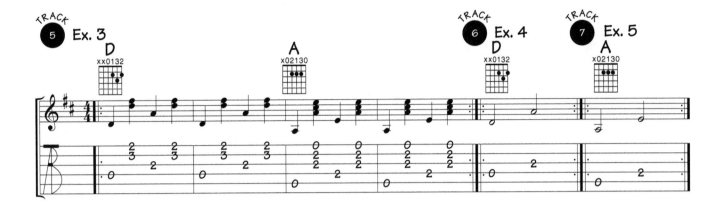

ALTERNATING BASS ON G

Let's move on to another chord. To play an alternating-bass strum on G, we're going to break our general rule about the second bass note: we're going to go up two strings, to the open fourth string, for our bass note on beat 3. It will sound like Example 6. Again, to troubleshoot: if that skip from the sixth to the fourth string is hanging you up, take out the strums and just play the bass notes, as in Example 7.

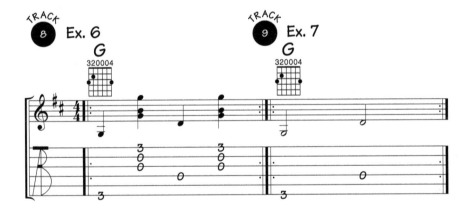

Let's make sure we can connect G to both D and A using alternating-bass strum patterns. First, try G to A and back in Example 8. From G to D involves a bit of a wrinkle: the upper bass note you play on beat 3 of a G chord, a D on the open fourth string, is the same note as you play on the first beat of the D chord. It may feel a little odd that in terms of bass notes, your picking hand is staying in the same place while your fretting hand is changing chords. But it sounds good: try it in Example 9.

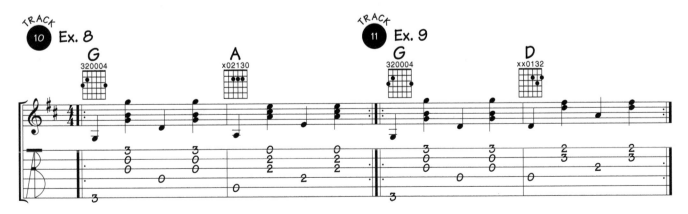

THE COMPLETE "COLUMBUS"

Let's play something with all three chords now. In Book 1, we played the *verse* to "Columbus Stockade Blues"; the *chorus* (the section that repeats, also known as the *refrain*) involves going to a G chord. Notice that the second half of the chorus uses the same chord progression as the verse we already know.

First try the chorus by itself, then put the whole song together: verse and chorus, all with alternating-bass strumming. Bring on the parking-lot jam session!

COLUMBUS STOCKADE BLUES

1. D
    WAY DOWN IN COLUMBUS, GEORGIA,
    A   D
    WANT TO BE BACK IN TENNESSEE

    WAY DOWN IN COLUMBUS STOCKADE
        A   D
    MY FRIENDS ALL TURNED THEIR BACKS ON ME

    G   D
    GO AND LEAVE ME IF YOU WISH TO
    G   A
    NEVER LET IT CROSS YOUR MIND
            D
    IF IN YOUR HEART YOU LOVE ANOTHER
    A   D
    LEAVE ME LITTLE DARLING I DON'T MIND

2.   D
    LAST NIGHT AS I LAY SLEEPING
        A   D
    I DREAMT I HELD YOU IN MY ARMS

    WHEN I AWOKE I WAS MISTAKEN
    A   D
    I WAS PEERING THROUGH THE BARS

        CHORUS

3.   D
    MANY A NIGHT WITH YOU I RAMBLED
        A   D
    MANY AN HOUR WITH YOU I SPENT

    THOUGHT I HAD YOUR HEART FOREVER
        A   D
    NOW I FIND IT WAS ONLY LENT

        CHORUS

LESSON 2
BLUES IN E

Let's add two more chords to our alternating-bass stash. For E, we'll follow our original rule: the first bass note is on the sixth string, and the second bass note is one string up, on the fifth string. That second note will be a B, at the second fret of the fifth string, on beat 3 (Example 1).

For B7, with its root on the fifth string, we'll also go up one string for the second bass note. On B7, that turns out to be a D♯, or the first fret on the fourth string (Example 2). A sharp symbol (♯) raises a note by a half step, or one fret. So a D♯ is one fret above the D note on the fourth string.

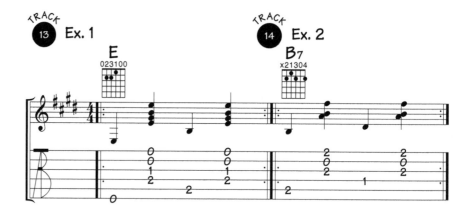

In Example 3, let's try making the move from E to A and back again with just one measure per chord, using an alternating-bass strum pattern. If this is moving too quickly for you, just back off and play two measures of each chord at first. Then, try two measures of one chord and one measure of the other, as in Example 4, where you play two measures of A followed by one measure of E and then repeat it.

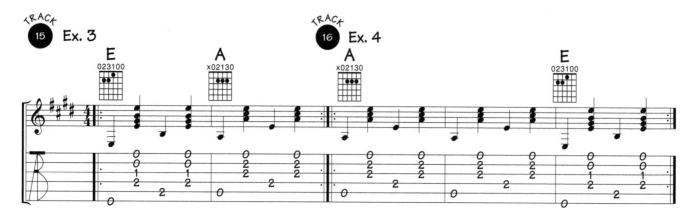

Now try the move from E to B7. Your right hand is doing the exact same moves as it did to switch from E to A: from bass notes on the sixth and fifth strings to bass notes on the fifth and fourth strings.

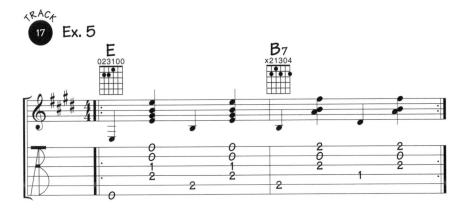

A CLASSIC BLUES

On to our next tune. With E, A, and B7 we're equipped to play the classic blues story-song "Stagolee." Note the quick switch from one bar of E up to B7 in measures 8–9. If it gives you any trouble, go back and spend a little more time with Example 5, which isolates that change.

ESSENTIAL LISTENING

Like "Careless Love," which we played in Book 1, **"Stagolee"** (also known as "Stack o' Lee Blues," "Stagger Lee," "Stackerlee," "Stack Lee" . . .) is one of those tunes that has appealed to jazz musicians as well as to blues singers. Sol Hoopii was a Hawaiian steel guitarist who played slide solos in a hot jazz style and influenced the role of the Dobro in bluegrass and country; he plays "Stack o' Lee" on *Master of the Hawaiian Guitar*, Vol. 1 (Rounder). Also check out Ma Rainey's early jazz version on *Ma Rainey's Black Bottom* (Yazoo). For the folk and blues side of things, try **Mississippi John Hurt**'s *1928 Sessions* (Yazoo), Woody Guthrie's *Muleskinner Blues: The Asch Recordings*, Vol. 2 (Smithsonian Folkways), or Tim and Mollie O'Brien's *Remember Me* (Sugar Hill).

STAGOLEE

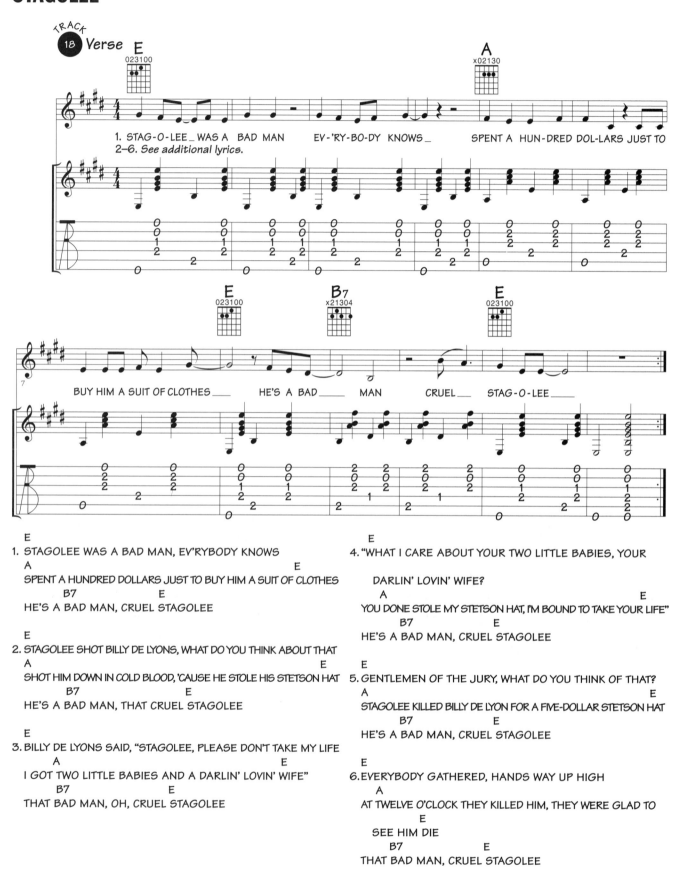

E
1. STAGOLEE WAS A BAD MAN, EV'RYBODY KNOWS
   A   **E**
   SPENT A HUNDRED DOLLARS JUST TO BUY HIM A SUIT OF CLOTHES
         B7   **E**
   HE'S A BAD MAN, CRUEL STAGOLEE

E
2. STAGOLEE SHOT BILLY DE LYONS, WHAT DO YOU THINK ABOUT THAT
   A   **E**
   SHOT HIM DOWN IN COLD BLOOD, 'CAUSE HE STOLE HIS STETSON HAT
         B7   **E**
   HE'S A BAD MAN, THAT CRUEL STAGOLEE

E
3. BILLY DE LYONS SAID, "STAGOLEE, PLEASE DON'T TAKE MY LIFE
   A   **E**
   I GOT TWO LITTLE BABIES AND A DARLIN' LOVIN' WIFE"
         B7   **E**
   THAT BAD MAN, OH, CRUEL STAGOLEE

E
4. "WHAT I CARE ABOUT YOUR TWO LITTLE BABIES, YOUR

   DARLIN' LOVIN' WIFE?
   A   **E**
   YOU DONE STOLE MY STETSON HAT, I'M BOUND TO TAKE YOUR LIFE"
         B7   **E**
   HE'S A BAD MAN, CRUEL STAGOLEE

E
5. GENTLEMEN OF THE JURY, WHAT DO YOU THINK OF THAT?
   A   **E**
   STAGOLEE KILLED BILLY DE LYON FOR A FIVE-DOLLAR STETSON HAT
         B7   **E**
   HE'S A BAD MAN, CRUEL STAGOLEE

E
6. EVERYBODY GATHERED, HANDS WAY UP HIGH
         A
   AT TWELVE O'CLOCK THEY KILLED HIM, THEY WERE GLAD TO
         E
   SEE HIM DIE
         B7   **E**
   THAT BAD MAN, CRUEL STAGOLEE

LESSON 3
MAJOR SCALES AND MELODIES

In Book I we learned a handful of melodies; now we're going to look at the *scales* that they're based on. A scale is a specific collection of notes, and you can think of them as containing the building blocks of melodies, much the way chords are the building blocks of a song's structure or chord progression. Let's learn a little bit about scales and then hear one at work in a traditional melody.

Like chords, scales can be major or minor (or have other qualities) and, also like chords, there's a scale for every letter in the musical alphabet. So there's a C-major scale, a D-major scale, an E-major scale, and so on, just as there is a C chord, a D chord, an E chord, and all the other ones you know. What does a scale sound like? Well, here's a C-major scale, which will probably sound pretty familiar:

TRACK 19 Ex. 1

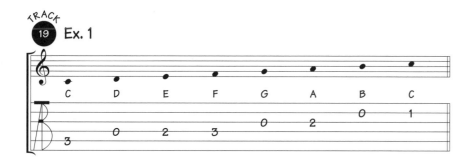

Notice that there's one note of every letter in the scale. It's a C scale because it starts and ends on C, but what makes it major? That has to do with the spaces between the notes. Take the same scale and play it all on one string, the fifth string.

TRACK 20 Ex. 2

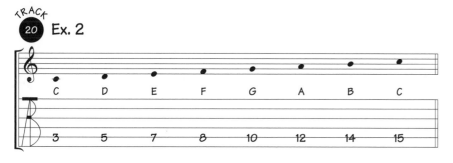

If you remember our discussion about half steps and whole steps in Book I, you can count which notes here are a whole step (two frets) apart and which notes are just a half step (one fret) apart. We get this pattern as we go up the scale: whole step, whole step, half step, whole step, whole step, whole step, half step. This is often abbreviated: W W H W W W H.

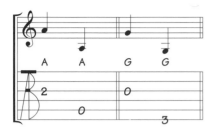

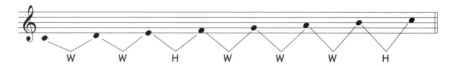

ESSENTIAL LISTENING

Back in Book 1, we played "Ida Red" and talked a little bit about Bob Wills and the Texas Playboys, the kings of western swing. **"The Girl I Left Behind Me"** was also in Wills' repertoire and can be heard on *The Tiffany Transcriptions,* Vol. 1 (Rhino). Also check out multi-instrumentalist Erik Darling's performance on *Instrumental Music and Songs of the Southern Appalachians* (Tradition), and for a bluegrass take, try Blue Highway's *It's a Long, Long Road* (Rebel).

We've already seen how you can play one note in more than one *register;* for example, we know how to play the note A on the open fifth string as well as at the second fret of the third string. Likewise, we've played G both at the third fret of the sixth string and at the open third string. Example 1 spells out a C scale in one octave, which runs from one C note to the next highest one. You could also play any of these notes, and this same scale, in another register—higher up the guitar neck. A melody that sticks to just these seven notes, whatever octave they are played in, is said to be in the key of C.

Here's a tune that illustrates this idea. "The Girl I Left Behind Me" is another traditional melody that lies well on the guitar, and in this arrangement all the notes are from the C-major scale. It includes two notes we mentioned, the A and G that are below the lowest C on the fretboard, as well as the low B (which we've learned as the bass note of a B7 chord). These notes are still in the C scale even though they're in a lower register than the one-octave version of the scale we know. Otherwise, all the notes lie within the one-octave scale of Example 1.

Alternate downstrokes and upstrokes for the eighth notes, as written; otherwise just use downstrokes.

THE GIRL I LEFT BEHIND ME

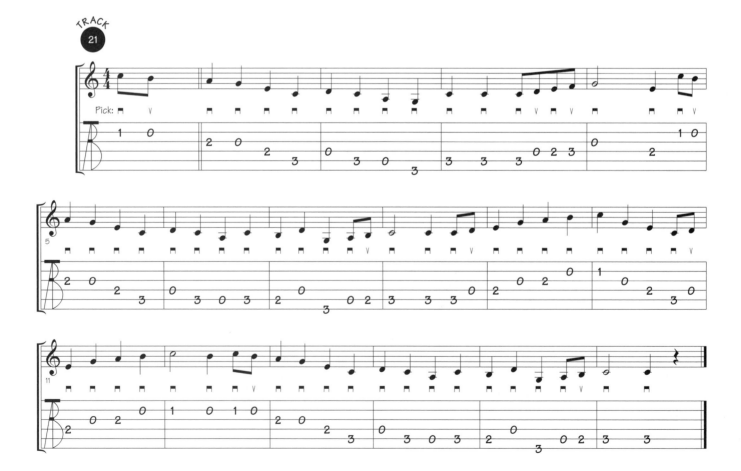

LESSON 4
STARTING TO FINGERPICK

So far we've been strumming and playing single notes with a pick (aka *flatpicking*), rather than our fingers. It's time to introduce *fingerstyle* or *fingerpicking* technique, which means that you literally pick the strings with your individual fingers and your thumb rather than with a pick. The great country blues, ragtime, and gospel guitarists were nearly all fingerpickers, with stylists like Mississippi John Hurt and Reverend Gary Davis exerting an enormous influence over subsequent generations of musicians. While flatpicking rules the bluegrass roost, there are exceptions (Lester Flatt, for one); meanwhile, two of the most influential fingerstylists come from the country tradition: Merle Travis and Chet Atkins.

We'll start by assigning the thumb and fingers to particular strings and use this idea to learn some basic *patterns*. Just as we learned to play one kind of strum pattern on several chords, we'll now take one way of fingerpicking the notes of a chord and learn how to switch between the various chords of a song while keeping the same pattern going. This idea is called (would you have guessed?) *pattern picking*.

GETTING IN POSITION

Let's start with a D chord. For our first pattern, we're going to use the index, middle, and ring fingers along with the thumb. Here's how these fingers are indicated in the notation:

p = thumb i = index m = middle a = ring

"Dave," I hear you say, "come on. *Thumb* starts with a *t*, not a *p*. And *ring* starts with an *r*, not an *a*. What's all this *p, i, m, a* stuff about?" Well, it comes from classical guitar notation, where *p* stands for *pulgar, i* stands for *indice, m* stands for *medio,* and *a* stands for *anular* (the Spanish words for thumb, index finger, middle finger, and ring finger). It takes a little getting used to, but this is how picking-hand fingerings are often indicated.

To start, rest your thumb on the fourth string, your index finger on the third string, your middle finger on the second string, and your ring finger on the first string.

Got that? Now, look at your fingers and thumb. You want to have your thumb about an inch closer to the fingerboard than your fingers, and your fingers should be somewhat curled up, without too big an arch to your wrist. If your fingers

Rest your thumb and fingers on the top four strings, then move your thumb closer to the fingerboard.

and thumb are all bunched together, try sliding your thumb along the strings toward the fingerboard as you slide your fingers back toward the bridge.

For now, your fingers are assigned to these strings: you're always going to use your thumb for the fourth string, index for the third, middle for the second string, and ring for the first string. To get used to this, lift your fingers from the strings as a group, then drop them back down onto the strings again. This is a lot like the exercise we did at the beginning of Book 1 to get used to landing your fingers together on a particular chord.

OK, now that you've gotten your fingers identified with the strings they're going to play, lift your hand up so your fingertips are hovering maybe half an inch above the strings. That's where you want to keep your hand when you play; if you leave your fingers resting on the strings, you'll keep those strings from ringing out.

FIRST PATTERN

On to the first pattern. You're going to just go up the strings, picking each string once, as in Example 1. Just think of it as rolling up the strings: thumb, index, middle, then ring. When that feels comfortable, try doing it two times in a row (Example 2).

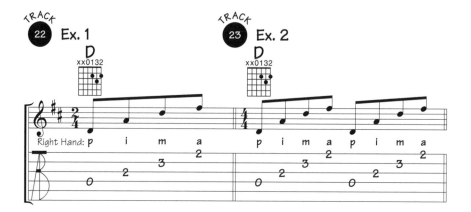

There it is: your first pattern. This is one of those things that basically just gets better with simple and constant repetition. Do it slowly enough to get every note sounding even and clear. Note: Unlike strumming, fingerpicking isolates every note of a chord, so it's kind of like a lie detector test for your left hand. You find out just how clearly—or not—you've been fretting your chords.

"Swell," I hear you say, "but Dave, how do I apply this pattern to, say, a C chord? Can I just change my left hand and let 'er rip?"

Well, almost. Keep your index, middle, and ring fingers on the same strings, but move your thumb down to the fifth string. Why? Well, this kind of pattern picking is like the first country backup bass/strum we did, in that you always want to pick out the root or bottom note of the chord on the first beat of the pattern. So, on a C chord, you could pick the fourth string with your thumb, because it's part of the chord, but the pattern will sound a lot fuller with a big fat C at the beginning. Like Example 3. To get used to repeating this pattern, try Example 4.

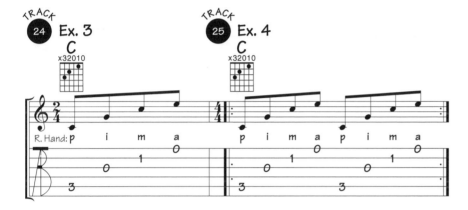

In Book I we learned the melody to "Shady Grove"; now let's play the chords using our first picking pattern. We'll need a new chord, too—D minor.

There's going to be a quick change between D minor and C in measure 7, where you have to play half a bar of the pattern on D minor and half a bar on C, then switch back to D minor again. To get used to that move, and to practice forming a D minor with your left hand, spend some time with these two exercises. In Example 5, play half a measure of D minor, then just the first note of the C pattern. In Example 6, play half a measure of D minor, half a measure of C, and then just the first note of the D pattern again.

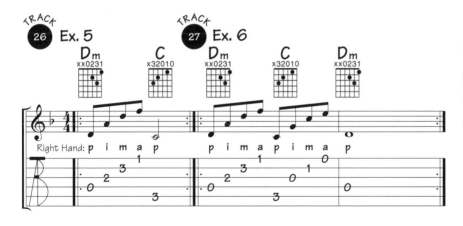

Now try the whole tune.

SHADY GROVE

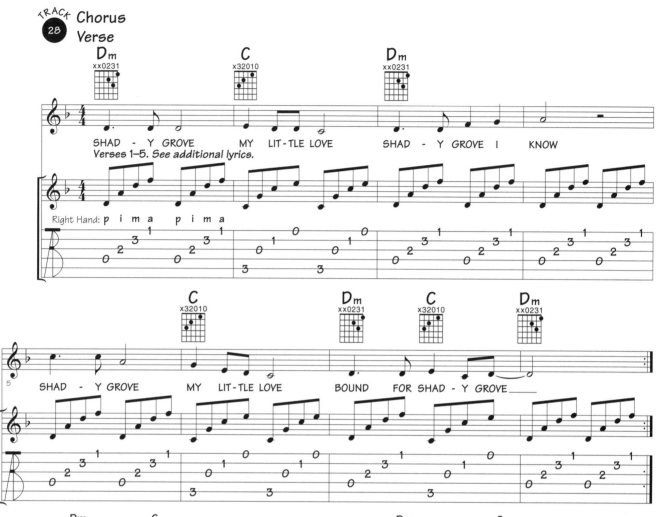

Chorus
Verse

SHAD - Y GROVE   MY LIT-TLE LOVE   SHAD - Y GROVE I KNOW
Verses 1–5. See additional lyrics.

Right Hand: p i m a   p i m a

SHAD - Y GROVE   MY LIT-TLE LOVE   BOUND FOR SHAD-Y GROVE____

Dm   C
SHADY GROVE MY LITTLE LOVE
Dm
SHADY GROVE I KNOW
              C
SHADY GROVE MY LITTLE LOVE
Dm   C   Dm
BOUND FOR SHADY GROVE

   Dm   C
1. I WISH I HAD A BANJO STRING
   Dm
   MADE OF GOLDEN TWINE
                 C
   EVERY TUNE I'D PICK ON IT
      Dm   C   Dm
   I'D WISH THAT GIRL WAS MINE

       CHORUS

   Dm   C
2. I WENT TO SEE MY SHADY GROVE
           Dm
   SHE WAS STANDING IN THE DOOR
                 C
   SHOES AND STOCKINGS IN HER HAND
       Dm   C   Dm
   AND HER LITTLE BARE FEET ON THE FLOOR

      Dm   C
3. I WISH I HAD ME A BIG FINE HORSE
              Dm
   AND THE CORN TO FEED HIM ON
                    C
   LITTLE SHADY GROVE TO STAY AT HOME
      Dm   C   Dm
   AND FEED HIM WHILE I'M GONE

       CHORUS

   Dm   C
4. PEACHES IN THE SUMMERTIME
   Dm
   APPLES IN THE FALL
                    C
   IF I CAN'T GET THE GIRL I LOVE
      Dm   C   Dm
   I DON'T WANT NONE AT ALL

      Dm   C
5. NOW WHEN I WAS A LITTLE BOY
           Dm
   I WANTED A BARLOW KNIFE
                    C
   AND NOW I WANT MY SHADY GROVE
      Dm   C   Dm
   TO SAY SHE'LL BE MY WIFE

LESSON 5
MORE PICKING PATTERNS

Let's apply our first fingerpicking pattern to a G chord. To do so, keep playing the top three strings with your index, middle, and ring fingers, but move your thumb all the way down to the sixth string, so that when we start the pattern on a G chord we've got a big low G in the bass:

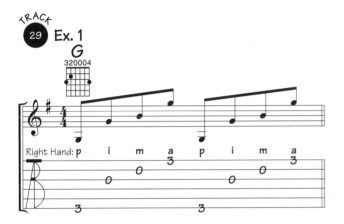

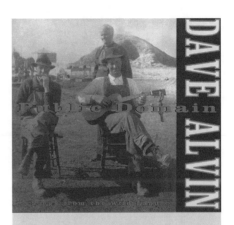

ESSENTIAL LISTENING

A tune like **"Shenandoah"** with such an enduring melody is bound to inspire instrumental as well as vocal versions. On the instrumental side, pick up bluegrass guitar master Tony Rice's *Unit of Measure* (Rounder), Nashville session ace Grady Martin's *Cowboy Classics* (Sony), or avant-roots jazzman Bill Frisell's *Good Dog, Happy Man* (Nonesuch). For vocals, consider Spider John Koerner's *Nobody Knows the Trouble I've Been* (Red House) or **Dave Alvin**'s *Public Domain* (HighTone).

Now the trick is going to be moving from chord to chord, bringing your thumb along to the right bass string while keeping your picking fingers the same on top. In Example 2, try switching between G and C. In Example 3, try switching between G and D.

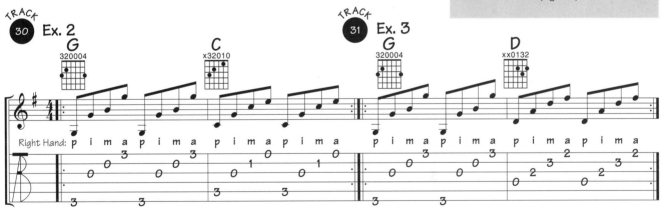

If your left hand is tripping you up as you try these new right-hand moves, leave the chords out for a moment: just practice making the right-hand pattern switches while playing the open strings. It will sound less than beautiful, perhaps, but it will let you focus on one thing at a time—in this case, bringing your thumb over to the right string. Then, when you feel like you're getting the hang of it, add the chords back in.

Let's use this picking pattern to play the lyrical old folk song "Shenandoah."

SHENANDOAH

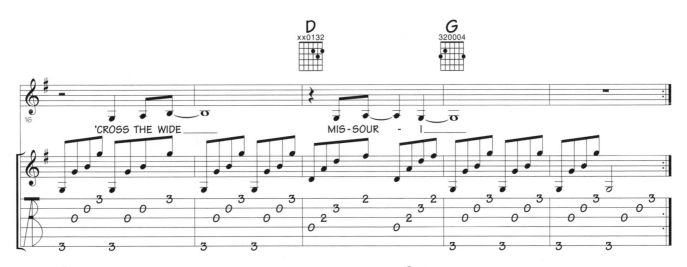

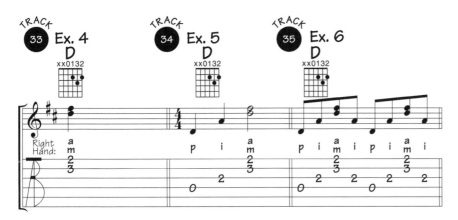

1.
 G
 SHENANDOAH, I LONG TO SEE YOU
   C   G
 AWAY, YOU ROLLING RIVER
 C   G
 SHENANDOAH, I LONG TO SEE YOU

 AWAY, BOUND AWAY
              D   G
 'CROSS THE WIDE MISSOURI

2.
 G
 SHENANDOAH, I LOVE YOUR DAUGHTER
   C   G
 AWAY YOU ROLLING RIVER
 C   G
 SHENANDOAH, I LOVE YOUR DAUGHTER

 AWAY, WE'RE BOUND AWAY
              D   G
 'CROSS THE WIDE MISSOURI

3.
 G
 SHENANDOAH, I LONG TO SEE YOU
   C   G
 AWAY, YOU ROLLING RIVER
 C   G
 SHENANDOAH, I'LL NOT DECEIVE YOU

 AWAY, WE'RE BOUND AWAY
              D   G
 'CROSS THE WIDE MISSOURI

4.
 G
 SEVEN YEARS, I'VE BEEN A ROVER
   C   G
 AWAY, YOU ROLLING RIVER
        C   G
 SEVEN YEARS I'VE BEEN A ROVER

 AWAY, BOUND AWAY
              D   G
 'CROSS THE WIDE MISSOURI

PATTERN NO. 2

Let's move on to another pattern. For this one, your middle and ring fingers are going to operate as a pair, picking the second and first strings simultaneously. In Example 4, try just that first, while fretting a D chord.

In Example 5, try rolling up the strings of a D chord by playing the thumb on the fourth string and then the index finger on the third string, followed by the second and first strings played together. And in Example 6, come back to the third string with your index finger after playing the top two strings together.

To move this pattern to an A chord, start your thumb on the fifth string while keeping your index, middle, and ring fingers on the top three strings, as in Example 7. For a G chord, keep your fingers in the same place while you bring your thumb down to the sixth string:

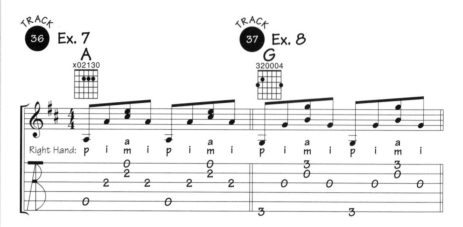

Example 7 includes a new note: C♯, at the second fret of the second string. We've actually been playing this note all along as part of an A chord but this is the first time we've had to read it. Remember the idea behind sharps: C♯ is the note you get when you raise a C one fret, or a half step. At the beginning Example 7, there's a ♯ symbol on the C and F spaces; this means that all C and F notes that follow are sharp. We'll talk more about this kind of notation when we continue our discussion of scales in the next lesson.

"CIRCLE" TIME

Practice these moves on the tune "Will the Circle Be Unbroken?"

WILL THE CIRCLE BE UNBROKEN?

D
WILL THE CIRCLE BE UNBROKEN
    G   D
BY AND BY, BY AND BY

THERE'S A BETTER HOME A-WAITING
        A   D
IN THE SKY, IN THE SKY

      D
1. I WAS STANDING BY THE WINDOW
     G   D
ON A COLD AND RAINY DAY

WHEN I SAW THAT HEARSE COME ROLLING
       A   D
FOR TO TAKE MY MOTHER AWAY

CHORUS

          D
2. WELL I TOLD THE UNDERTAKER
       G   D
UNDERTAKER, PLEASE DRIVE SLOW

FOR THAT BODY YOU'RE A-CARRYING
          A   D
WELL I HATE TO SEE IT GO

CHORUS

LESSON 6
THE G-MAJOR SCALE

And now, dig through your pockets or between the cushions of the couch for one of those little plastic triangles, because we're going to resume playing with a pick in this lesson. In Lesson 3, we talked about the fact that there's a formula for the major scale: you start and end on the same note, play one of every note in between, and always have the same combination of half steps and whole steps between notes. Before we go ahead and try making a G-major scale, we'll need to learn a couple more notes on the fingerboard: F and G on the first string.

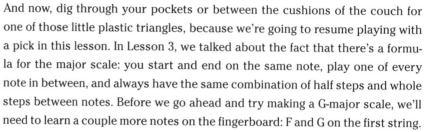

We were introduced to the E on the first string back when we learned the six open strings of the guitar; it's shown on the top space of the staff. F is always a half step or one fret up from E, so in this case it's found at the first fret of the first string and shown on the top line of the staff. G is a whole step or two frets up from F, so it's played at the third fret on the first string and shown just above the top line of the staff.

Now let's play one of every note from G on the third string to a G on the first string and see if it sounds like a G scale:

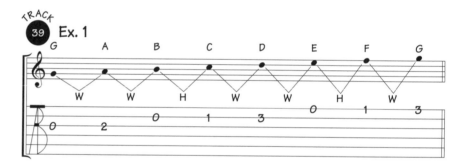

If you sing the familiar "do re mi fa sol la ti do" to this scale, you may notice that it sounds a little off toward the end. Let's count the half steps and whole steps and see if they fit our formula of W W H W W W H. From G to A is two frets, or a whole step; from A to B is also two frets, another whole step. B to C on the second string is a half step, then C to D and D to E are also whole steps. So far, so good. But now, E to F is a half step, where, according to the formula, we should have a half step. And then to end things, F to G is two frets, or a whole step, and that doesn't fit either.

What's the story? To make this a normal major scale, we need a way to create the correct order of whole and half steps. Raising the seventh note, F, a half step, makes the pattern fall into place. The name for an F note raised a half step is F sharp (F♯), and it's shown on the staff by putting a ♯ symbol in front of the F note itself. F♯ is a half step higher than F, so it's played at the second fret of the first string.

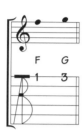

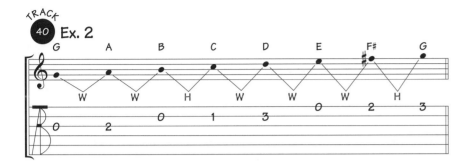

Using this F♯ in place of F, we've got the right arrangement of whole steps and half steps in our G-major scale. And if you listen to the scale with the F♯, you'll hear that it has that "do re mi" scale sound all the way up to the top.

Here's a tune in the key of G that makes use of all the notes of this G-major scale. Note that we use a ♯ symbol at the beginning of each staff. This tells you to play every F note that follows as an F♯. Since doing so will create a melody in the key of G, this notation is called a *key signature.* There is a different key signature for every key.

The accompaniment part on the CD uses this pattern:

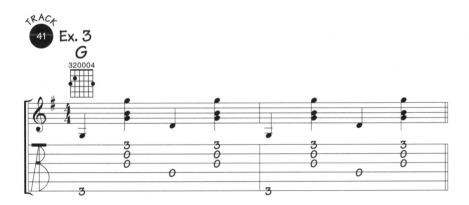

ESSENTIAL LISTENING

The **Holy Modal Rounders** are a perfect example of how you can get away with all kinds weirdness if you have the knowledge and the chops to back it up. The duo of fiddler Peter Stampfel and guitarist Steve Weber coalesced in the Greenwich Village folk scene in the early '60s, and while they clearly knew their old-time music, they didn't hold it sacred. Made-up verses and a careening, almost out-of-control performance style were par for the course, as was a repertoire that ranged from "Statesboro Blues" to "Clinch Mountain Backstep." Hear all that *and* their version of **"Sail Away Ladies"** on the Holy Modal Rounders' collection *1 & 2* (Fantasy).

The Rounders' setting of this tune borrows heavily from the classic version made popular by the first Grand Ole Opry star, Uncle Dave Macon. You can hear his rendering on *Go Long Mule* (County). On the *Anthology of American Folk Music* (Smithsonian Folkways) there's Uncle Bunt Stephens' unaccompanied version, recorded in 1926. The New Lost City Ramblers play "Ladies" on *Old Time Music* (Vanguard). Legendary Appalachian fiddler Tommy Jarrell does a wicked version on *The Legacy of Tommy Jarrell,* Vol 1: *Sail Away Ladies* (County).

SAIL AWAY LADIES

LESSON 7
BASS RUNS

We've already learned how to play a steady *boom-chick* bass/strum with an alternating bass; now it's time to add in some *bass runs*. A bass run is a short phrase, usually just two or three notes long, that helps to lead from one chord into another. For example, here's a bass run into G:

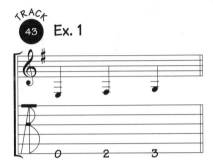

Before we get into how to use this run, notice that it introduces a new note, the low F♯ at the second fret on the sixth string. We've had F♯ on the first string already, and finding F♯ on the sixth string works the same way: it's a half step, or one fret, from E to F, so when you raise F a half step (one fret) to F♯, you're now a total of a whole step (two frets) up from E.

To play this bass run, you want to start so that when you land on the third note, G, it's actually the first bass note of our bass/strum pattern. So you count off as in Example 2. As you may remember from Book 1, this kind of phrase is called a *pick-up*. Example 3 shows the bass run leading into two full measures of G.

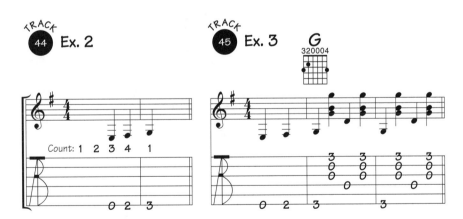

"OK," you're probably thinking, "that's cool, but what if I want to play this bass run again after a couple of measures of G?" Right. Well, all you've really got to do is take out the last two beats of the second full measure of G—one bass and one strum—and drop in the first two notes of the bass run, E and F♯.

Starting right on the downbeat, it will sound like Example 4. If you start with the bass-run pickup and just keep going in G, throwing the bass run in every two measures, it sounds like Example 5.

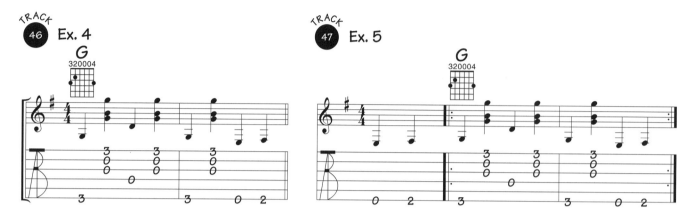

As they said in my high school French class, "Très cool, n'est pas?" Meaning, if I recall correctly, "Very cool, is it not?"

Now, since there are very few songs that have the consideration to just sit on a G chord the entire time, what we really want to do is use this bass run to get back to G from various other chords, like C and D for starters. So try Example 6: play two measures of alternating bass/strum on a D chord, but drop out the last bass/strum to play the bass run back up to G. Then in Example 7, add in a full two measures of G bass/strum.

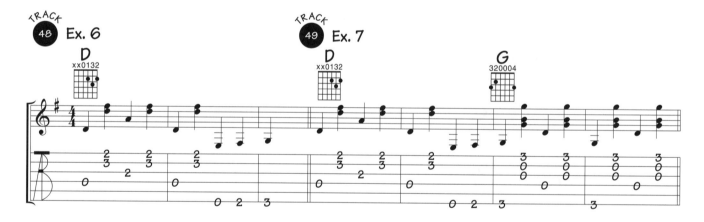

Before we go from a C chord to a G with the bass run, we'll need an alternating-bass pattern to play on a C chord. Start with the C on the fifth string, third fret, for the first bass note and go up to the fourth string, second fret (E), for the upper bass note.

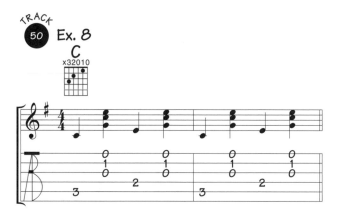

Next, just like we did on the D chord, take out the last bass/strum before going to the G, and drop in the bass run: E, F♯, G. Try it in Example 9. Then try going from C into the bass run and then playing two full measures of G with an alternating bass/strum (Example 10).

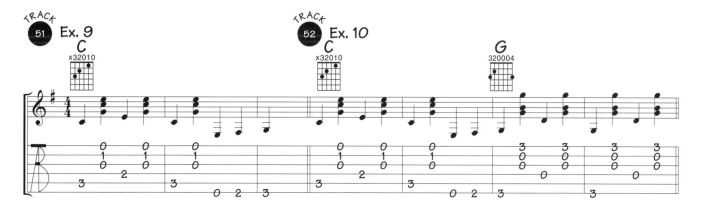

Let's put all this to use in "I Am a Pilgrim." The song is in the key of G, but you start on a D chord. Every time the G comes around, you get into it using the bass run, except in measure 14, where you've only got one measure of D before getting back to the G chord. Notice also that in measures 8–9, you play the bass run in the middle of a four-measure stretch of G, not unlike what we practiced in Example 5.

ESSENTIAL LISTENING

Merle Travis' *Folk Songs of the Hills* (Capitol), originally issued on a set of four 78-rpm records in 1947, featured the ground-breaking fingerstyle guitarist in a solo acoustic setting, doing traditional tunes and soon-to-be-standard originals like "Sixteen Tons" and "Dark as a Dungeon" as well as the expected folk material like **"I Am a Pilgrim."** Travis also pioneered the use of the electric guitar in country music, wrote western swing classics like "Smoke! Smoke! Smoke! That Cigarette" and clever wordplay tunes like "Divorce Me C.O.D.," and, with Paul Bigsby, helped develop a custom solid-body instrument that anticipated the design of Leo Fender's Telecaster. Speaking of which, check out the Byrds' version on their country-rock salvo *Sweetheart of the Rodeo* (Legacy); Byrds guitarist Clarence White can be heard playing the tune in another setting on *The Kentucky Colonels Featuring Clarence White* (Rounder).

I AM A PILGRIM

D   G
1. I AM A PILGRIM AND A STRANGER
        C   G
TRAV'LING THROUGH THIS WORRISOME LAND
                   C
I'VE GOT A HOME IN THAT YONDER CITY
    G D   G
AND IT'S NOT, NOT MADE BY HAND

D   G
2. I'VE GOT A MOTHER, SISTER, AND BROTHER
        C   G
WHO HAVE GONE, GONE ON BEFORE
                              C
AND I'M DETERMINED TO GO AND MEET THEM
    G D   G
OVER ON THAT OTHER SHORE

LESSON 8
MORE BASS RUNS

If you're thinking there must be a way to play a bass run into other chords besides G, you're right. The bass run into C looks a lot like the bass run in G moved up a string (which makes sense, considering how much the bottom notes of a C chord look like those of a G chord moved up one string). Here it is: the notes A, B, and C.

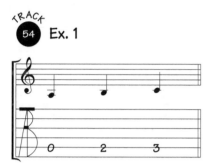

Like the G bass run, the C bass run starts two beats before the 1 of a bass/strum pattern. The third note of the C bass run, C, becomes the first bass note of a C bass/strum, as in Example 2.

If you want to just hang on a C chord, throwing in the bass run every other time, drop out the second bass/strum in the second measure of the pattern and replace it with the first two notes of the bass run, A and B (Example 3).

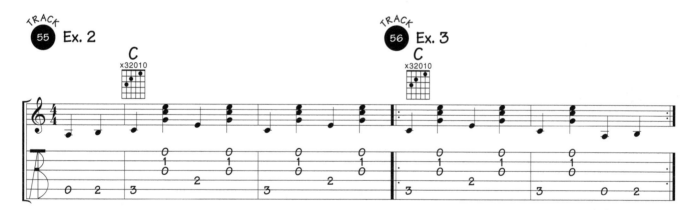

Try switching between C and G now, using a bass run every other measure to get into the next chord. In Example 4, you start on a pickup measure with a bass run up to a C chord, then halfway through measure 2 you play the G bass run into measure 3. At the end of measure 4, you play the C bass run up into the C chord, and keep going around like that.

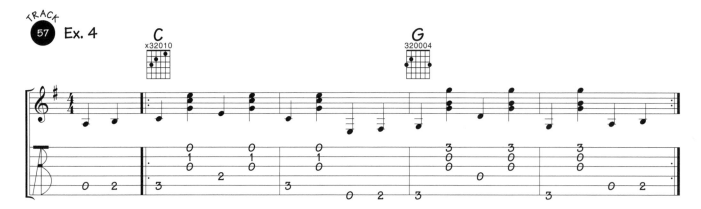

TRACK 57 Ex. 4

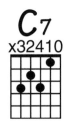

C7
x32410

Let's add these moves into "I Am a Pilgrim." While we're at it, we'll add a couple of seventh chords to the arrangement as well. You already know G7, and we'll use it here to create more motion during the four bars of G in the middle of the tune, strengthening the transition up to C in the process. The C7 in measures 5–6 and 11–12 is a new chord. To play it, you put down your fingers for a regular C chord and then add in your pinky at the third fret of the third string.

This chord is a kind of optional sound—use it if you like it. You can hear a particularly tasteful use of the seventh-chord sound on David Grisman and Tony Rice's instrumental version of this tune, recorded on the first *Tone Poems* CD (Acoustic Disc). Here's "I Am a Pilgrim" with seventh chords added and bass runs into both G and C.

I AM A PILGRIM

TRACK 58 Verse

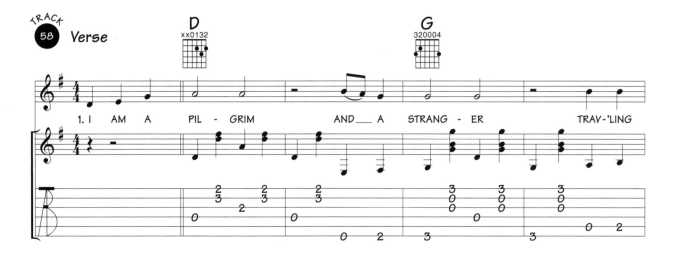

1. I AM A PIL-GRIM AND ___ A STRANG-ER TRAV-'LING

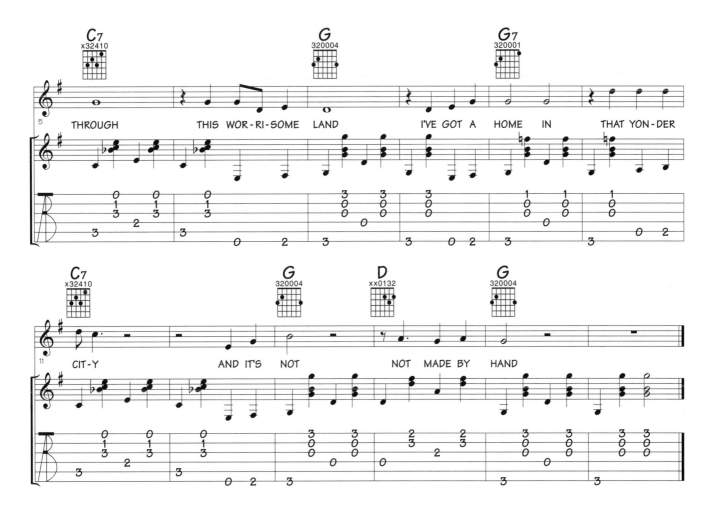

THROUGH   THIS WOR-RI-SOME LAND   I'VE GOT A   HOME   IN   THAT YON-DER

CIT-Y   AND IT'S   NOT   NOT   MADE BY   HAND

D BASS RUNS

How you play a bass run into a D chord depends on whether you're playing in the key of G or the key of D. Either way, you'll have to start on a fretted note, ending up on the open fourth string, which is the root of the D chord.

Let's do a bass run that works in the key of D. The notes of this run include another new note on the fretboard, a C# on the fifth string. C# is one fret, or a half step, above the C we've just been playing at the third fret, so you'll find C# at the fourth fret.

Example 5 shows the notes for the D bass run. In Example 6, the third note of the bass run, D, becomes the first bass note of a bass/strum pattern on D.

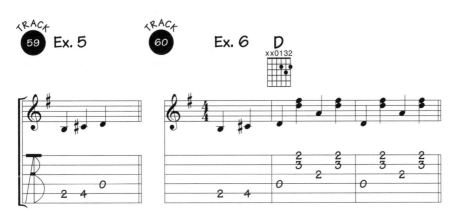

TRACK **59** Ex. 5

TRACK **60** Ex. 6   D

When you play a bass run into G or C, your ring finger is landing on the bottom note you need to fret for the chord you're about to play. It's almost as if the bass run is helping you get your fingers in place. Going into a D chord, playing the bass run doesn't help you get any of your fingers into the right place for the chord itself. However, the first note of a D-chord bass/strum pattern is the open D on the fourth string, so you have a whole beat free in which to get your fingers into place over on the top three strings. Also, as you finish the bass run, your index finger will have just been at the second fret of the fourth string, so it only has to come over one string, to the second fret of the third string, to be in place for the D chord.

In Example 7, practice staying on a D chord, dropping in the bass run every other time in place of the last bass/strum of the second measure. Then, in Example 8, try switching between a D and a G using a bass run into each chord.

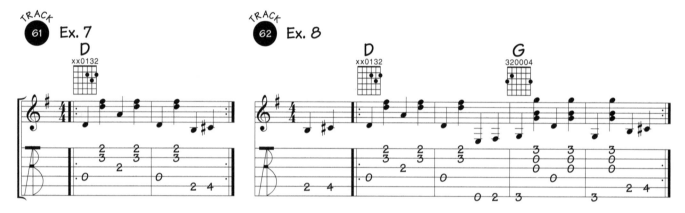

PLAY IT

"Bury Me Beneath the Willow" is in the key of D, and we'll play it with bass runs into D and into G.

ESSENTIAL LISTENING

"Bury Me beneath the Willow," a particularly plaintive tale of unrequited love, has been recorded by many artists, past and present. Woody Guthrie plays it on *The Early Years* (Legacy); western swing bandleader Spade Cooley can be heard holding forth with a small group on *Radio Broadcasts 1945* (Country Routes). Modern flatpicker Tony Rice and mandolinist Ricky Skaggs included the tune on their duet record *Skaggs and Rice* (Sugar Hill), and for an instrumental version, investigate guitarist **Scott Nygaard**'s solo debut *No Hurry* (Rounder).

BURY ME BENEATH THE WILLOW

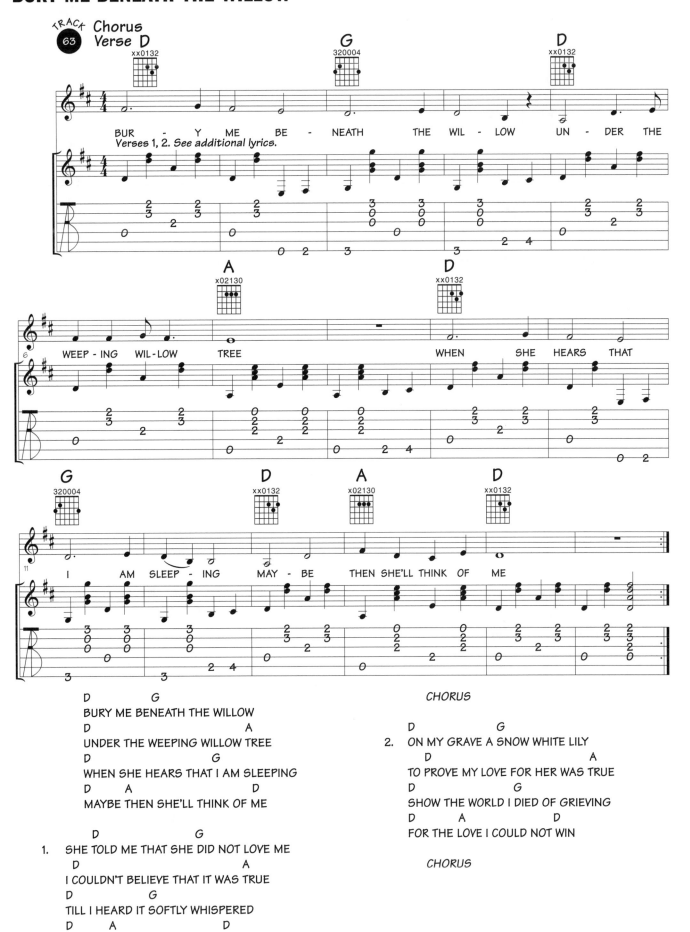

D   G
BURY ME BENEATH THE WILLOW
D   A
UNDER THE WEEPING WILLOW TREE
D   G
WHEN SHE HEARS THAT I AM SLEEPING
D   A   D
MAYBE THEN SHE'LL THINK OF ME

          D   G
1. SHE TOLD ME THAT SHE DID NOT LOVE ME
      D   A
  I COULDN'T BELIEVE THAT IT WAS TRUE
  D   G
  TILL I HEARD IT SOFTLY WHISPERED
  D   A   D
  SHE NO LONGER CARES FOR YOU

          CHORUS

      D   G
2. ON MY GRAVE A SNOW WHITE LILY
        D   A
  TO PROVE MY LOVE FOR HER WAS TRUE
  D   G
  SHOW THE WORLD I DIED OF GRIEVING
  D   A   D
  FOR THE LOVE I COULD NOT WIN

          CHORUS

LESSON 9
BLUES BASICS

E7
020100

The blues is many things: a genre, a repertoire, a feel and a sensibility, and a form. As a genre, blues covers a dizzying variety of styles and artists; as a repertoire, it includes thousands of tunes both traditional and composed; the blues feeling and sensibility is a significant part of how musicians approach everything from jazz and rock to bluegrass and swing; and the 12-bar blues form is a cornerstone of all of those styles as well.

What do we mean by *form,* anyway? We've played fiddle tunes with an AABB form, where each A and each B section is eight bars long. There are many forms used in the blues repertoire, but the classic blues is 12 bars long and has the form AAB, where each section is four bars long. We've already encountered a version of the blues form in Lesson 2, with the tune "Stagolee." In the key of E, one of the simplest 12-bar blues has this chord progression:

 TRACK **64** Ex. 1
12-Bar Blues Progression

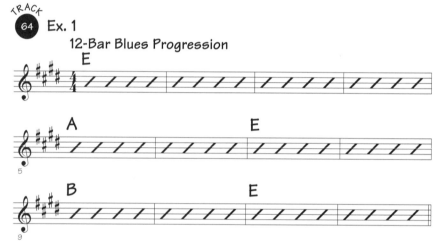

A7
x02030

The AAB description comes as much from the arrangement of the lyrics as the chords, because the first line (A) is repeated before being answered in the B. And as you can see, there is actually some variation between the chords of the first and second A section.

One of the distinguishing sounds of the blues is the use of seventh chords for all three chords of the progression. We already know how to play a B7, so we'll need to add E7 and A7 to our chord stash. These are actually easy to learn, because for both of them, you just leave one note *out* of the regular chord.

To play an alternating bass/strum pattern on E7, remember to use the sixth string for the first bass note and the fifth string for the second bass note, just as you do on a regular E chord. And you can use the same alternating bass/strum pattern for A7 as you do for A.

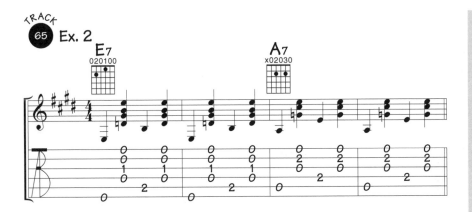

BLUES RIFFS

Another characteristic of the blues is that sometimes a single blues phrase, or *riff,* will work with more than one chord. For example, start with the bass run in Example 3. The new note, G♯, is a half step (or one fret) above the G we know and love at the third fret of the sixth string. The natural sign (♮) next to the first note shows that this G is *not* sharp.

Now, we can use this bass run to kick off a bass/strum on an E7 chord, as in Example 4. We can use it to hang on an E7 chord for more than two bars, as in Example 5. We can use it to get from an E7 chord up to an A7 chord, as in Example 6, or to get from an A7 back down to E7, as in Example 7.

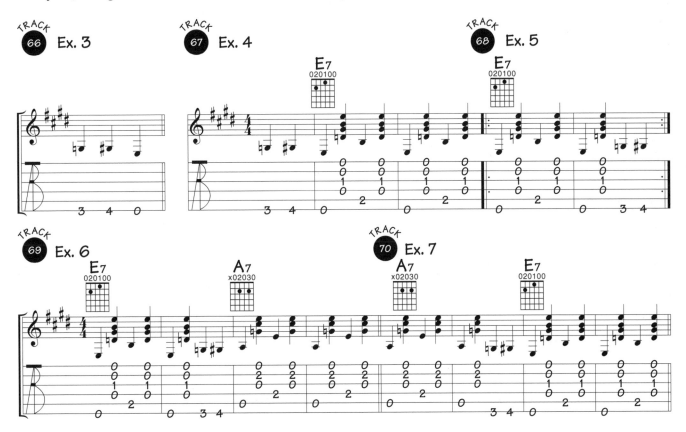

PLAY IT

Try out all these ideas in our next song, "Alberta," a 12-bar blues.

ALBERTA

	E	E7
1.	OH ALBERTA, WHERE'D YOU STAY LAST NIGHT?	
	A7	E
	OH ALBERTA, WHERE'D YOU STAY LAST NIGHT?	
	B7	E
	CAME HOME THIS MORNING, THE SUN WAS SHINING BRIGHT	

	E	E7
2.	IF YOU DON'T LOVE ME, WHY DON'T YOU TELL ME SO?	
	A7	E
	IF YOU DON'T LOVE ME, WHY DON'T YOU TELL ME SO?	
	B7	E
	I'M BROKENHEARTED, WITH NO PLACE TO GO	

	E	E7
3.	OH ALBERTA, WHERE YOU BEEN SO LONG?	
	A7	E
	OH ALBERTA, WHERE YOU BEEN SO LONG?	
	B7	E
	AIN'T HAD NO LOVIN' SINCE YOU'VE BEEN GONE	

LESSON 10
ALTERNATING-BASS FINGERPICKING

By now you may have noticed that picks are slippery things. No matter how many you start out with, you quickly lose all but one, which you then cling onto for weeks on end, wondering why you couldn't keep track of the previous half dozen the same way. Eventually they turn up in twos and threes at the bottom of the washing machine, where, presumably, they've been hanging out with all the single, unmatched socks. Who needs it?

So let's drop the pick again and add the alternating-bass sound into a fingerpicking pattern. To keep things simple, we'll start with a picking pattern we already know, the one from Lesson 5. The bass notes that we use on the various chords won't be any different from what we've been playing in the last several songs, but now we'll be playing those bass notes with our thumb instead of a pick.

Here's how it works. On an E chord, our basic fingerpicking pattern goes like Example 1. When we do an alternating-bass/strum on an E chord now, we play Example 2. Combining the alternating bass from Example 2 with the picking pattern of Example 1, we get Example 3.

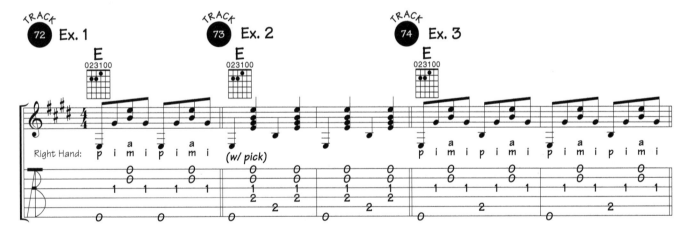

All we've basically done is borrow the upper bass note—the B at the second fret of the fifth string—and substituted it for the low E of the picking pattern, every other time. So now, instead of hitting E with our thumb every time, we hit E then B, E then B.

We can use the same idea on A, alternating the thumb between the fifth string and the fourth string as in Example 4. Once you can do that, your right hand doesn't change at all to play over a B7 chord; in Example 5, your thumb still alternates between the fifth string and the fourth string.

Now, practice these alternating-bass picking patterns over pairs of chords so that you can switch back and forth between E and A (Example 7) and between E and B7 (Example 8). Make sure you maintain the pattern in your right hand and hit the correct bass notes.

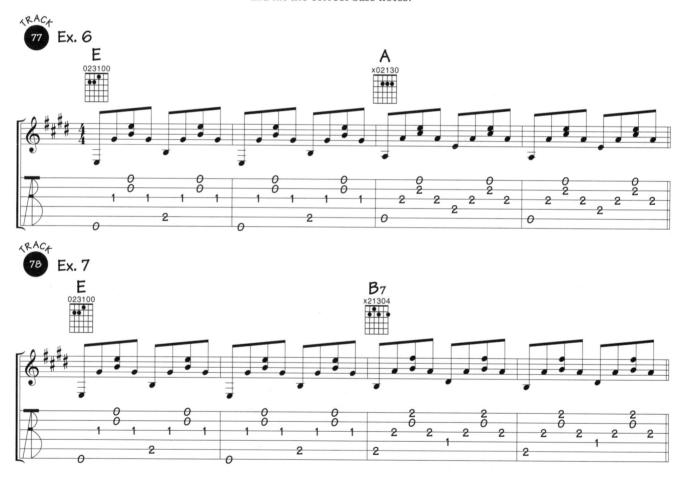

Now here's a tune to play with this alternating-bass picking pattern: "Sugar Babe."

SUGAR BABE

Verse
TRACK 79

1. SUG-AR BABE____ I'M TIRED OF YOU____ AIN'T YOUR LOV-ING BUT THE WAY____YOU DO____
2–4. See additional lyrics.

SUG-AR BABE____ IT'S ALL O-VER NOW____

	E			E	
1.	SUGAR BABE, I'M TIRED OF YOU		3.	SUGAR BABE, WHAT'S THE MATTER WITH YOU	
	A			A	
	AIN'T YOUR LOVIN' BUT THE WAY YOU DO			YOU DON'T TREAT ME LIKE YOU USED TO DO	
	E B7 E			E B7 E	
	SUGAR BABE, IT'S ALL OVER NOW			SUGAR BABE, IT'S ALL OVER NOW	
	E			E	
2.	ALL I WANT MY SUGAR TO DO		4.	SUGAR BABE, I'M TIRED OF YOU	
	A			A	
	MAKE FIVE DOLLARS AND GIVE ME TWO			AIN'T YOUR HONEY BUT THE WAY YOU DO	
	E B7 E			E B7 E	
	SUGAR BABE, IT'S ALL OVER NOW			SUGAR BABE, IT'S ALL OVER NOW	

ESSENTIAL LISTENING

"Sugar Babe" is generally associated with Mance Lipscomb, a farmer and songster from Navasota, Texas, whose first name was short for "Emancipation." Listen to his performance on *Texas Songster* (Arhoolie); for an East Coast version, pick up Pink Anderson's *Ballad and Folk Singer*, Vol. 3 (Original Blues Classics). British folk guitarist John Renbourn's take can be heard on various reissues of his early work, including *John Renbourn/Another Monday* (Castle), and back in the States, check out old-time fiddler Bruce Molsky's *Bruce Molsky and Big Hoedown* (Rounder).

LESSON 11
FINGERPICKING IN 3/4

For our last lesson in Book 2, let's take a look at how our two main picking patterns can be adapted to play tunes in 3/4. We'll start with an E-minor chord and work our way up to the folk-blues classic "House of the Rising Sun."

The first pattern we learned, in Lesson 4, really lasts for only two beats if you just play it once: thumb, index, middle, ring. On an E-minor chord, that sounds like Example 1. To make it work in waltz time, or 3/4, we need to add one more beat. We can get that by coming back down the strings at the end, repeating the second and third strings with the middle and index fingers (Example 2). Try playing this pattern for a few measures in a row, as in Example 3.

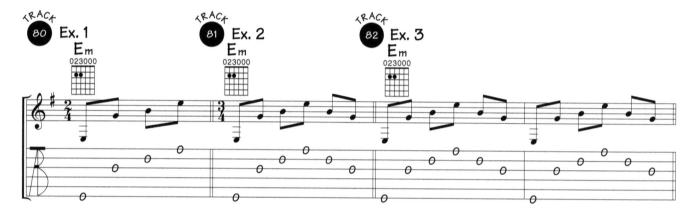

In Example 4, try it on a G chord. You can keep your picking hand on the same strings—sixth, third, second, and first. To play on an A-major chord (Example 5) or a C-major chord (Example 6), bring your thumb up to pick the fifth string, and keep your index, middle, and ring fingers on the top three strings. Example 7 shows this pattern on a B7 chord.

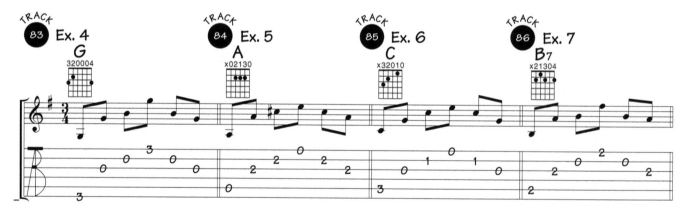

"HOUSE" RULES

"House of the Rising Sun" requires you to switch chords every bar, except in measures 7 and 8, when you hang on the B7 for two bars. In particular, we've never switched between A and C before, so you might want to isolate that change, as in Example 8:

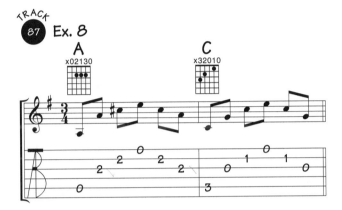

It's a good idea to practice making one-bar switches back and forth between each pair of chords: E minor to G and back, G to A and back, A to C and back, G to B7 and back, B7 to E minor and back.

On page 44 you'll find the entire tune. For the CD, it has been recorded using a capo at the fifth fret, making this arrangement in the key of E minor *sound* in the key of A minor. You can play the song in E minor just the way it's written out, without the capo, if that's a good key for your voice. But if you want to sing in a higher key or practice along with the CD (many recorded versions of "House" are also in the key of A minor), place your capo at the fifth fret and keep everything else the same: play the exact same chords with the exact same picking pattern.

ESSENTIAL LISTENING

In this day and age it's well nigh impossible to hear the phrase "house of the rising sun" without experiencing a sudden aural flash: those rippling electric arpeggios that kick off the Animals' now-definitive version of the tune from 1964, available on *The Complete Animals* (EMI). But by the time the British Invasion band got its hands on **"House of the Rising Sun,"** it had been around for a long, long time; originally it was sung from a woman's point of view. It all makes a lot more sense that way, since the Rising Sun of the song was essentially a brothel, something New Orleans had in great abundance until the Storyville red-light district was shut down in 1917. That's how Dylan cut it on his first record, *Bob Dylan* (Columbia); his arrangement owed a lot to Dave Van Ronk, who later did it on *Just Dave Van Ronk* (Mercury, out of print). **Tony Rice**'s *Unit of Measure* (Rounder) includes a strong instrumental rendition.

HOUSE OF THE RISING SUN

```
       Em G        A         C
1.   THERE IS A HOUSE IN NEW ORLEANS
       Em      G     B7
THEY CALL THE RISING SUN
          Em       G      A        C
AND IT'S BEEN THE RUIN OF MANY A POOR GIRL
        Em     B7      Em    B7
AND ME, I KNOW I'M ONE
```

```
         Em      G     A      C
2.   MY MOTHER WAS A TAILOR
        Em          G        B7
SHE SEWED THESE NEW BLUE JEANS
        Em       G     A        C
MY SWEETHEART WAS A GAMBLER
     Em    B7        Em    B7
DOWN IN NEW ORLEANS
```

```
           Em  G      A        C
3.   NOW THE ONLY THING A GAMBLER NEEDS
        Em     G      B7
IS A SUITCASE AND A TRUNK
          Em  G       A      C
AND THE ONLY TIME HE'S SATISFIED
     Em        B7     Em  B7
IS WHEN HE'S ON A DRUNK
```

```
       Em     G     A       C
4.   GO TELL MY BABY SISTER
       Em     G     B7
NEVER DO LIKE I HAVE DONE
       Em      G        A       C
BUT SHUN THAT HOUSE IN NEW ORLEANS
        Em    B7     Em  B7
THEY CALL THE RISING SUN
```

```
         Em      G     A        C
5.   IT'S ONE FOOT ON THE PLATFORM
        Em     G      B7
THE OTHER'S ON THE TRAIN
       Em  G      A       C
I'M GOING BACK TO NEW ORLEANS
        Em        B7      Em      B7
TO WEAR THAT BALL AND CHAIN
```

```
         Em      G     A        C
6.   I'M GOING BACK TO NEW ORLEANS
        Em     G      B7
MY RACE IS ALMOST RUN
       Em       G        A         C
I'M GOING TO SPEND THE REST OF MY LIFE
        Em     B7     Em   B7
BENEATH THE RISING SUN
```

CONGRATULATIONS

You've made it through the second book of *The Acoustic Guitar Method*! We've covered a lot of ground—alternating-bass strums, bass runs, fingerpicking patterns, new chords, new scales, and of course, plenty of new tunes. As you may be realizing by now, each new chord, strum, or pattern you learn is both useful on its own and as a building block for what's coming next. Even as you play through these songs just for the enjoyment of it, you're solidifying your foundation, getting ready for what lies ahead in Book 3 and beyond. So take your time and let it all soak in. As you check out some of the recommended listening, feel free to start sorting out what you like best from the rest. And as always, no matter how wrapped up you get in it all, don't forget to pick up the guitar just because.

THE
ACOUSTIC
GUITAR
METHOD

3

WELCOME

Greetings, guitarist! You've made it through Books 1 and 2—are you feeling the healthy, self-righteous glow of accomplishment? No? Well, just think about it: you may have tender fingertips right now, but you've also got a big handful of tunes under those fingertips, and you can play them with alternating-bass strums, assorted cool bass runs, and various fingerpicking patterns. Take a look at the summary of Book 2 below to remind yourself how far you've come, and then get ready for even more as we move ahead.

In Book 3, we'll learn some new alternating-bass strums with a swing feel, discover some new bass notes to play, and take on the essential fingerpicking technique known as Travis picking. We'll also check out the left-hand moves known as hammer-ons, pull-offs, and slides and learn how adding intros and endings to a tune really make it sound complete. And as always, we'll do all this while learning more great songs from the American roots repertoire.

 Introduction — TRACK 1

Tune-Up — TRACK 2

WHAT WE LEARNED IN BOOK 2

Chords

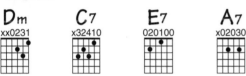

Alternating Bass with Strums

Bass Runs

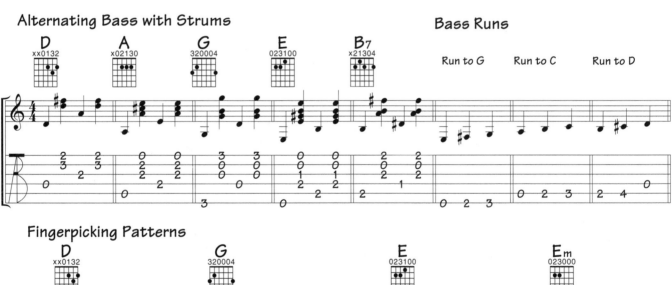

Fingerpicking Patterns

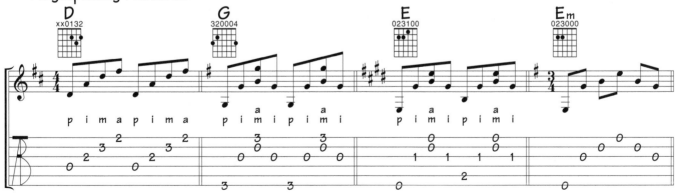

LESSON 1
THE SWING FEEL

Let's begin by learning a technique that gives a lot of roots music—blues in particular—its special rhythmic drive. In short, let's make the music swing.

In Book 1 and Book 2, we played all of our songs and examples with what's called a *straight-eighth-note feel*. This means that whether we did a strum that was all eighth notes (as in Book 1) or a fingerpicking pattern that was all eighth notes (as in Book 2), the notes were all played evenly and held for the same amount of time: a straight count of "1 and 2 and 3 and 4 and . . ."

"Well," I hear you say, "that's how it's supposed to be, right?" Well, yes, but not always. There's also something called *swing eighth notes*. Swing eighth notes, or *swing eighths,* have a more lilting feel than straight eighths; the first of each pair of notes is given a little more weight than a regular eighth note, and the second note is given a little less. The first eighth note is actually held a little longer than a straight eighth note, and the second note is a little shorter. Sound confusing? Pop in the CD and compare the recording of Example 1, in which the chords are strummed with a straight-eighths feel, to Example 2, in which the chords are strummed with a swing-eighths feel. Listen for the difference, and then try playing the strum both ways yourself:

BEAT BY BEAT

As you look at the notation in Example 3, remember that an arrow pointing up indicates a *downstroke* (toward the floor) and an arrow pointing down indicates an *upstroke* (toward the ceiling). Strums are written this way to be consistent with the notation and tablature, in which the lowest-pitched notes are at the bottom and highest-pitched notes are on top. Here's what's happening, beat by beat:

1	Pick the low A bass note
and	
2	Strum a downstroke on the top strings
and	Strum an upstroke on the top strings
3	Pick the upper bass note, E
and	
4	Strum a downstroke on the top strings
and	Strum an upstroke on the top strings

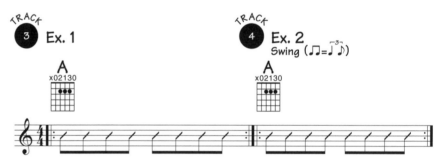

Now let's spruce up our alternating-bass pattern by adding some strums on the upper strings. We'll add in an upstroke after each strum on the upper strings. Try Example 3, which uses an A chord. Each pair of strums on top has a swing-eighth feel. In Example 4, try playing just the strums on top, to get that ragged long-short rhythm.

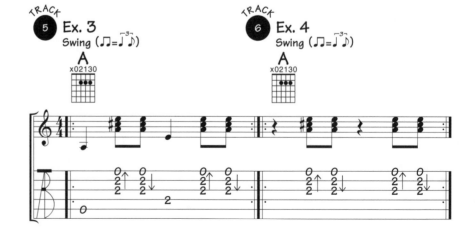

In Example 5, try the new pattern on a D7 chord. The only difference will be that your bass notes are played on the fourth and third strings instead of on the fifth and fourth strings. The next couple of examples will help you practice keeping this pattern going while switching between chords: in Example 6, between A and D7, and in Example 7, between A and E7. When you're comfortable with all these moves, try them out in the tune "Frankie and Johnny" on page 8.

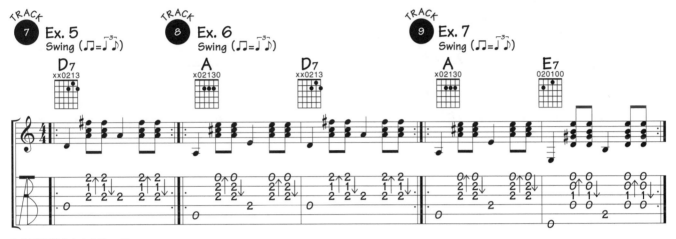

PATTERN NO. 2

By slipping in another upstroke just after each bass note, we can get a whole other strum pattern going using the swing-eighths feel. It sounds like this:

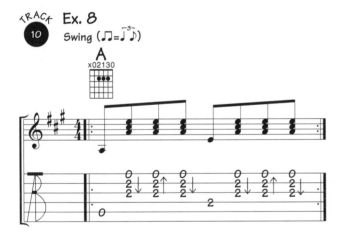

This pattern requires a light touch, for the high strings anyway. (You may want to revisit the discussion in Book 1 on holding the pick for strumming upstrokes and downstrokes.) The trick is to get a good *thwack* at the bass note, then go sailing over the rest of the strings to come in for an upstroke on the high strings, all within the space of an eighth note's time. Try exaggerating the movements of your picking hand—really pick *out* from the face of the guitar into space on the bass notes, then come circling back in to get that first upstroke.

When you've got Example 8 under your fingers, try playing through "Frankie and Johnny" with this second strum pattern.

FRANKIE AND JOHNNY

1. FRANKIE AND JOHNNY WERE SWEETHEARTS

                                       A
   OH HOW THEY COULD LOVE
   D7
   SWORE TO LOVE ONE ANOTHER
                               A
   UNDERNEATH THE STARS ABOVE
               E   A
   HE WAS HER MAN, HE WAS DOING HER WRONG

2. FRANKIE WENT DOWN TO THE CORNER SALOON

                                       A
   TO GET A BUCKET OF BEER
   D7
   SAID TO THE BARTENDER
                                 A
   "HAS MY LOVIN' MAN BEEN HERE?
              E   A
   HE'S MY MAN, BUT HE'S DOING ME WRONG"

       A

3. "AIN'T GONNA TELL YOU NO STORIES

    I AIN'T GONNA TELL YOU NO LIES
     D7
    I SAW THAT MAN ABOUT AN HOUR AGO
                A
    WITH A GIRL NAMED NELLIE BLIGH
           E   A
    HE'S YOUR MAN, BUT HE'S DOING YOU WRONG"

       A

4. FRANKIE WENT DOWN TO THE HOTEL

    DIDN'T GO THERE FOR FUN
     D7
    FRANKIE WENT DOWN TO THE HOTEL
                A
    WITH A LOADED FORTY-FOUR GUN
           E   A
    HE WAS HER MAN, BUT HE WAS DOING HER WRONG

       A

5. FRANKIE LOOKED OVER THE TRANSOM

    TO SEE WHAT SHE COULD SPY
     D7
    THERE SAT JOHNNY ON THE SOFA
                A
    JUST LOVING UP NELLIE BLIGH
           E   A
    HE WAS HER MAN, BUT HE WAS DOING HER WRONG

       A

6. FRANKIE GOT DOWN FROM THAT HIGH STOOL

    DIDN'T WANT TO SEE NO MORE
     D7
    ROOT-DE-TOOT, THREE TIMES SHE SHOOT
                   A
    RIGHT THROUGH THAT HARDWOOD DOOR
           E   A
    HE WAS HER MAN, BUT HE WAS DOING HER WRONG

       A

7. "OH ROLL ME OVER EASY

    ROLL ME OVER SLOW
     D7
    ROLL ME OVER ON THE RIGHT SIDE BOYS
                   A
    FOR THE LEFT SIDE HURTS ME SO"
           E   A
    HE WAS HER MAN, BUT HE WAS DOING HER WRONG

       A

8. DARK WAS THE NIGHT

    COLD WAS THE GROUND
     D7
    THE LAST WORDS I HEARD FRANKIE SAY
                A
    "I DONE LAID OLD JOHNNY DOWN
           E   A
    HE WAS MY MAN, BUT HE WAS DOING ME WRONG"

ESSENTIAL LISTENING

"Frankie and Johnny" was one of two Mississippi John Hurt songs included on Harry Smith's *Anthology of American Folk Music* (Smithsonian Folkways), and it had a huge impact on folk-revival guitarists. According to Dave Van Ronk, everyone tried to master Hurt's dazzling fingerpicking on the tune, with rare success. When Hurt was rediscovered in the 1960s, he didn't play "Frankie" as fast as on his 1928 recording, and when Van Ronk delicately inquired why that might be, Hurt revealed that the original version had been sped up considerably in order to fit it onto a 78-rpm record. **Bob Dylan** plays this tune as "Frankie and Albert" on his collection of traditional songs *Good As I Been to You* (Columbia).

LESSON 2
TACKLING THE F CHORD

Use the first joint of your index finger to fret the top two strings.

Yes, the time has come to learn the potentially difficult but very necessary F chord. It'll take some time and effort to get it sounding clear, but once you do, you'll be able to play a whole batch of new songs. Our first F is played on the top four strings and looks a little bit like a crumpled-up C chord.

What makes the F chord challenging is the way you've got to hold down the top two strings with just your index finger. You may find yourself wanting to pull your whole hand around and under the neck of the guitar to get your index finger flat across the two high strings. If you do this, you'll be pulling your middle and ring fingers flat across the strings, muting the same strings you're trying so hard to press down. Also, any time you shift the whole angle of your hand and wrist, you make it harder and more time consuming to either get back to another chord or get to the F chord in the first place.

"So, Mr. Smarty Book Writer," you ask, "just how *am* I supposed to make this chord happen?"

Well, it is a little tricky, but what you've basically got to do is flatten out the first joint of your index finger, making a little bar across those top two strings, while keeping your middle and ring fingers arched or squared so that they come in cleanly on just the notes they're supposed to grab, clearing all the surrounding strings. It may help you to think about keeping your thumb braced at the back of the neck.

In Example 1, try playing the F with the first of the two strum patterns we just learned in Lesson 1. Your first bass note will be on the fourth string, and your second bass note will be on the third string. Then practice going back and forth between C and F, as in Example 2. As you do so, focus on getting your fingers into each chord in time without slowing down your strumming hand. If you can deal with the muted, plucky sound you get at first and keep going, you *will* get there in time.

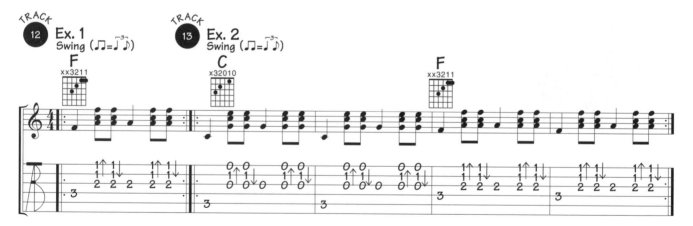

Now let's try a new strum pattern. It's like doing a regular bass/strum for the first two beats of a measure and the busier bass/up-down-up pattern we used on "Frankie and Johnny" for the second two beats. Try it first on just a C chord (Example 3), using an open G on the third string for the upper bass note. Next, try the same pattern on an F chord (Example 4), and then practice switching between C and F (Example 5).

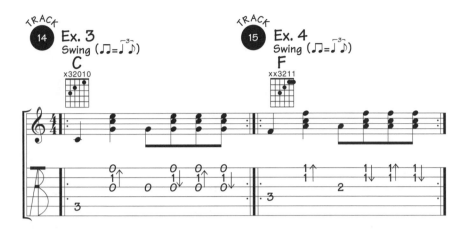

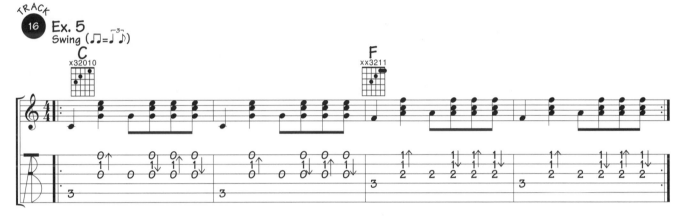

BLUES IN C

The song "Delia" is our first song to include an F chord. It's 12 bars long and loosely follows the blues form, with an interesting way of hanging on the F in the second line. Take it at a relaxed tempo.

ESSENTIAL LISTENING

Twelve-string guitarist **Blind Willie McTell** is best known as the composer of "Statesboro Blues," but the Atlanta guitarist had a career that lasted, with ups and downs, from the prewar era to the edge of the folk revival—he made his last recordings three years before his death in 1959. You can hear his version of **"Delia"** on *The Essential Blind Willie McTell* (Classic Blues). Country blues scholar and performer Stefan Grossman turns in his rendition on *Shake That Thing: Fingerpicking Country Blues* (Shanachie); Roy Book Binder's early solo release *Travelin' Man* (Adelphi) includes a version as well.

DELIA

1.
```
    C
DELIA WAS A GAMBLING GIRL
        F        C                        F
DELIA WAS A GAMBLING GIRL BUT SHE'S LAID HER

        MONEY DOWN
    C        G            C
SHE'S ALL I'VE GOT AND GONE
```

2.
```
    C
DELIA, WHY DIDN'T YOU RUN?
        F                    C
WHEN CUTTER CAME CHASING AFTER YOU WITH THAT
        F
        FORTY-FOUR GUN?
    C        G            C
SHE'S ALL I'VE GOT AND GONE
```

3.
```
    C
DELIA'S MAMA WEEP, AND DELIA'S DADDY MOAN
        F                    C
THEY WOULDN'T HAVE HATED IT SO BAD IF ONLY
        F
        DELIA HAD DIED AT HOME
    C        G            C
SHE'S ALL I'VE GOT AND GONE
```

4.
```
    C
A RUBBER-TIRED CARRIAGE, AND A DOUBLE-SEATED HACK
            F                    C
CARRIED DELIA DOWN TO THE GRAVEYARD BUT THEY
        F
        DIDN'T BRING HER BACK
    C        G            C
SHE'S ALL I'VE GOT AND GONE
```

5.
```
    C
DELIA, HOW COULD IT BE
                F                C
YOU COULD LOVE ALL THOSE GAMBLING MEN BUT YOU
        F
        NEVER COULD LOVE ME
    C        G            C
SHE'S ALL I'VE GOT AND GONE
```

LESSON 3
MORE CHORD MOVES

In this lesson we'll look at switching to F from a couple of other chords and tackle the idea of switching chords every two beats while keeping a pattern going. Why all this work? For the payoff, baby—if we can do all these things, we'll be able to play a very excellent tune called "Gambler's Blues," also known as "St. James Infirmary."

First, let's use the new strum pattern from Lesson 2 to play an A-minor chord (Example 1). Then let's see about switching to F from A minor. In Example 2, play one bar of each with the same strum.

The first note you need to hit when you switch from A minor to F is the root note, F, so you want to take care of that first, with your ring finger. Your middle finger stays at the same fret but moves over one string. And your index finger is the anchor, staying at the first fret of the second string for both chords. If you're having trouble with this switch, break it down into the steps at right.

When you've got that working somewhat, try switching from F to E, as in Example 3. This is a little trickier. Every finger has to move, but your ring finger at least stays on the same string, so move it first. See the step-by-step breakdown.

MINOR MOVES

We haven't had both A minor and E in the same song yet, but as you may recall, they look very similar. To switch between A minor and E, just lift all three of your fingers together and move them as a group: down one string to E or up one string to A minor. In Example 4, try those moves with the same strum pattern we've been using, with one bar of each chord.

Let's take this all one step further by learning how to play two chords in one measure, or switching between A minor and E every two beats. As far as the picking goes, there won't be any upper bass notes to play, because we'll just have time to play the first bass note of each chord, followed by strums on the high strings, before switching to the next chord and playing *that* chord's first bass note. Check out Example 5 to hear what it sounds like.

STEP BY STEP

Am to F

1. Move your ring finger from the second fret on the third string to the third fret on the fourth string.

2. Sneak your middle finger one string higher, from the second fret of the fourth string to the second fret of the third.

3. Without lifting it off the second string, flatten your index finger to cover both the second string and the high string at the first fret.

F to E

1. Slide your ring finger back one fret (to the second fret), staying on the fourth string.

2. Move your middle finger over to the fifth string, second fret.

3. Move your index finger over one string, to the third string, still at the first fret.

When you switch from E back to F, slide your ring finger back up to the third fret. If you do this first, you'll be sure to have the root of the chord, F, in place for when you go to pick your first bass note on F. Meanwhile, you can be getting your index and middle fingers in place.

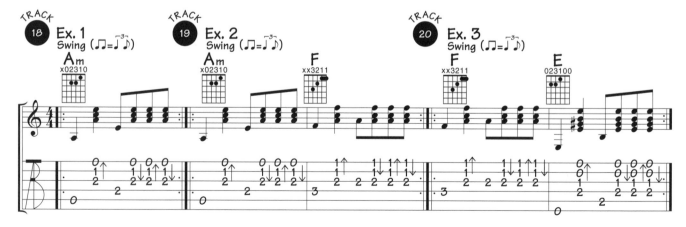

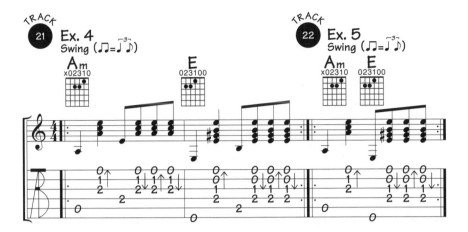

If these moves are giving you trouble, break them down first, as in Example 6. Hit the bass note and strums for A minor and then just move your hand over to the E chord. Don't worry about the strums. Then play the A-minor bass/strums again. Next, in Example 7, do the same thing but hit the E bass note on beat 3. Then try the full bass/strum in Example 8.

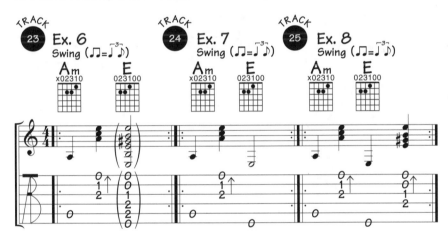

In Example 9, try the same thing starting on E: play the E bass/strum and just move your hand over to A minor for two beats. And finally, in Example 10, do the same thing as Example 9 but add in the A bass note when you get to the A-minor chord.

We'll need a few other quick changes to play our next tune. Try switching from A minor to D minor in Example 11, and from F to E in Example 12. If you find either of these particularly difficult, break down the change into steps, the same way we did for switching from A minor to E.

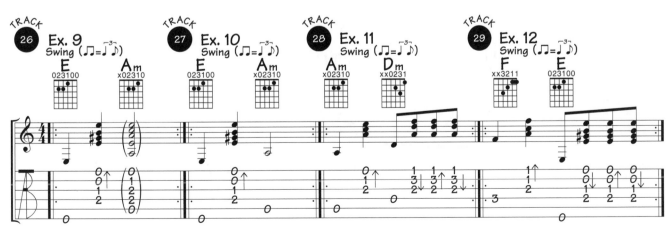

PLAY IT

Let's put this all together in the tune "Gambler's Blues." If you want to simplify things as you're learning the song, you can leave out the upstrokes and use the basic bass/strum pattern shown in Example 8.

GAMBLER'S BLUES

```
        Am      E       Am
1.  IT WAS DOWN BY OLD JOE'S BARROOM
                    F        E
    ON THE CORNER BY THE SQUARE
        Am      E       Am    Dm
    THEY WERE SERVING DRINKS AS USUAL
        F       E           Am    E
    AND THE USUAL CROWD WAS THERE


        Am      E       Am
2.  ON MY LEFT STOOD BIG JOE MCKENNEDY
                    F        E
    HIS EYES WERE BLOODSHOT RED
        Am      E       Am    Dm
    HE TURNED TO THE CROWD AROUND HIM
                F       E       Am    E
    THESE WERE THE VERY WORDS THAT HE SAID


        Am      E           Am
3.  I WENT DOWN TO THAT ST. JAMES INFIRMARY
                    F        E
    AND I SAW MY BABY THERE
        Am      E       Am    Dm
    STRETCHED OUT ON A LONG WHITE TABLE
    F       E           Am    E
    SO SWEET, SO COLD, SO FAIR


        Am      E       Am
4.  LET HER GO, LET HER GO, GOD BLESS HER
                F        E
    WHEREVER SHE MAY BE
        Am      E           Am    Dm
    SHE MAY SEARCH THE WIDE WORLD OVER
            F       E           Am    E
    AND NEVER FIND ANOTHER MAN LIKE ME
```

```
        Am      E       Am
5.  WHEN I DIE, WHEN I DIE PLEASE BURY ME
                    F        E
    IN MY HIGH-TOPPED STETSON HAT
        Am          E           Am        Dm
    PUT A TWENTY DOLLAR GOLD PIECE ON MY WATCH CHAIN
                F           E           Am    E
    SO MY FRIENDS WILL KNOW I DIED STANDING PAT


        Am      E       Am
6.  GET ME SIX GAMBLERS TO BEAR MY COFFIN
                    F        E
    SIX CHORUS GIRLS TO SING ME A SONG
        Am          E       Am        Dm
    PUT A TWENTY-PIECE JAZZ BAND ON MY TAILGATE
            F       E       Am    E
    TO RAISE HELL AS I ROLL ALONG


        Am      E       Am
7.  LET HER GO, LET HER GO, GOD BLESS HER
                F        E
    WHEREVER SHE MAY BE
        Am      E           Am    Dm
    SHE MAY SEARCH THE WIDE WORLD OVER
                F       E           Am    E
    AND NEVER FIND ANOTHER MAN LIKE ME


        Am          E       Am
8.  WELL, NOW THAT I'VE TOLD MY STORY
                    F        E
    LET'S HAVE ANOTHER ROUND OF BOOZE
        Am    E       Am    Dm
    AND IF ANYONE SHOULD ASK YOU
            F       E       Am    E
    WELL, I'VE GOT THOSE GAMBLER'S BLUES
```

ESSENTIAL LISTENING

Folk-blues revivalist **Dave Van Ronk** included **"Gambler's Blues"** on his very first recording, the 1959 Folkways LP *Dave Van Ronk Sings Ballads, Blues, and a Spiritual*; that material is now available on *The Folkways Years* (Smithsonian Folkways). Pioneering jazz trumpeter and singer Louis Armstrong recorded the tune early on as "St. James Infirmary Blues," and you can hear his 1928 version on *The Louis Armstrong Collection, Vol. 4: Louis Armstrong and Earl Hines* (Columbia). Mance Lipscomb's "St. James Infirmary" is included on the documentary video *A Well Spent Life* (Flower Films), and the Boston-based Tarbox Ramblers recorded the tune on their self-titled 2000 debut (Rounder).

LESSON 4
INTRODUCING TRAVIS PICKING

Man with the golden thumb: Merle Travis.

It's time to learn the most essential fingerpicking approach in roots music, known generally as *Travis picking* (after Merle Travis, who popularized it) or the *alternating thumb* (or *alternating bass*) style. We had a picking pattern in Book 2 that involved an alternating bass played by the thumb on the first and third beats; with Travis picking, you hit a lower bass note on the first and third beat of each bar, and an upper bass note on the second and fourth beat of each bar—or a bass note on every beat. (Travis picking is basically only done in 4/4 time.) So on an A chord, your thumb is going to bounce back and forth between the fifth string and the fourth string, as in Example 1.

Once you've got your thumb going, your fingers are each going to be assigned to a particular string, just as they were for the fingerpicking patterns we learned in Book 2. For our first Travis picking pattern, your index finger (notated, remember, as *i*) is assigned to the third string. Pick the third string with your index finger right after you pick the lower bass string with your thumb. Every time you hit that fifth string with your thumb, follow it up with your index finger on the third string, as in Example 2.

Your middle finger (notated as *m*) is assigned to the second string. Pick the second string with your middle finger right after you pick the *upper* bass string (the fourth string) with your thumb. So every time you hit the fourth string with your thumb, follow it up with your middle finger on the second string, as in Example 3.

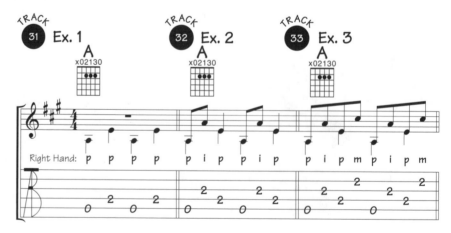

That's the whole pattern. Take it really slowly at first, going through these stages one at a time until you're sure your thumb is alternating correctly every time and your fingers are following the right thumb notes on the right strings. Then gradually increase your speed, keeping everything solid and even as you do.

PICKING ON E

Let's try this pattern on another chord, E. Your fingers are going to stay assigned to the same strings, but your thumb will now alternate between the

---

PRACTICE TIP

When you're learning these patterns, it's tempting to pick very lightly on the strings so it's not as obvious if you make a mistake. The secret to playing a really grooving Travis pattern, however, is digging in and playing with conviction. So here's Dave's Practice Advice: Close the door, go outside, or wait till nobody's home, and then play this pattern as slowly—and as *loudly*—as you can. Really pick each note, really commit to making it ring out, and do it slowly enough that there's no doubt what note you're trying to play. Do this a little bit every time you work on a pattern like this, and you'll start to feel the difference.

sixth string and the fourth string, as in Example 4. In Example 5, bring in the index finger on the third string after every bass note on the sixth string. Finally, in Example 6, add in your middle finger on the second string after every bass note on the *fourth* string.

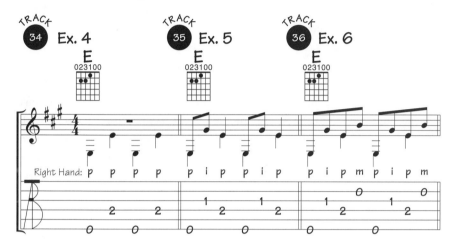

When the E chord is starting to feel as solid as the A chord, try switching back and forth between the two. It may help to practice just playing the different bass notes while you change chords (Example 7), then bringing in your index and middle fingers (Example 8).

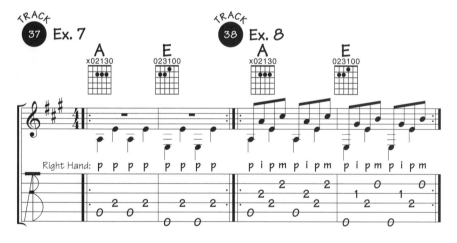

THE BIG D

When you're fingerpicking and playing four particular strings, you can get away with using certain chord *voicings* (arrangements of the notes) that wouldn't work if you were strumming across all six strings. Here's a version of a D chord that sounds great for fingerpicking. You can finger this chord a couple of different ways, as shown in the photos and chord diagrams.

This is like a standard D chord, only we've taken the F♯, the second fret on the high string, and moved it to the bass, at the second fret on the sixth string. That gives us a much deeper-sounding version of D, written as D/F♯ and pronounced "D over F sharp," which means "a D chord on top with an F♯ note underneath it." It doesn't matter that we're no longer fretting the high string, because we aren't going to pick it anyway (as indicated by the *X* in the chord diagram).

CAPO TRICK

Note that in Book 1 we played "Banks of the Ohio" in the key of G—now we're playing it in the key of A. You actually *can* play the melody as we learned it along with our new Travis-picking part: just put a capo at the second fret and follow the tab in Book 1—the capo raises the melody from the key of G up to A. This is a great trick to use for a guitar duet: in this instance, one player could use A fingerings without a capo, while the other uses G fingerings with a capo at the second fret. The two positions create different sounds that harmonize perfectly together.

One of the fingerings shows that you use your thumb for the low F♯. That's not a typo! Many folk, blues, jazz, and rock guitar players use this technique for this D shape and other chords: you reach up around the back of the neck and pin down the sixth string with the fleshy part of the first joint of your thumb. The version with just your fingers works equally well here, so try them both and pick the one that's most comfortable for you. The thumb technique is worth working on, because down the line it will come in handy to have one more finger freed up to play other notes with.

In Example 9, apply our Travis-picking pattern to this chord using the same finger-to-string assignments as for an E chord: thumb on the sixth and fourth strings, index on the third string, middle on the second string. In Example 10, practice the switch between A and D/F♯. Your index and middle fingers will do the same thing in both examples, and your upper bass note will stay the same. Only your low bass note will change, from the fifth string for A to the sixth string for D/F♯.

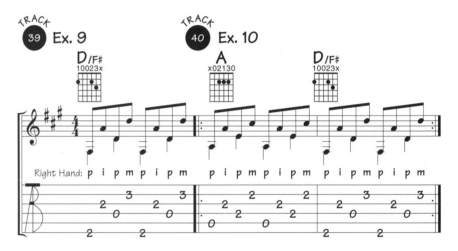

Let's use these three chords, A, E, and D/F♯, to revisit "Banks of the Ohio," which we first played back in Book 1.

BANKS OF THE OHIO

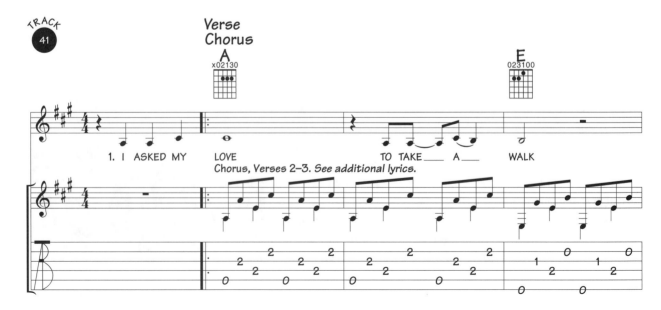

1.   A   E
    I ASKED MY LOVE TO TAKE A WALK
           E7   A
    TAKE A WALK, JUST A LITTLE WALK
        A7   D/F#
    DOWN BESIDE, WHERE THE WATERS FLOW
              A   E   A
    DOWN BY THE BANKS OF THE OHIO

           A   E
    AND ONLY SAY THAT YOU'LL BE MINE
           E7   A
    AND IN EACH OTHER'S ARMS ENTWINE
        A7   D/F#
    DOWN BESIDE, WHERE THE WATERS FLOW
              A   E   A
    DOWN BY THE BANKS OF THE OHIO

2.   A   E
    I HELD A KNIFE UP AGAINST HER BREAST
           E7   A
    AS INTO MY ARMS SHE PRESSED
              A7   D/F#
    SHE CRIED OH WILLIE, DON'T YOU MURDER ME
              A   E   A
    I'M NOT PREPARED FOR ETERNITY

    CHORUS

3.   A   E
    I STARTED HOME, 'TWEEN TWELVE AND ONE
           E7   A
    I CRIED MY GOD, WHAT HAVE I DONE
              A7   D/F#
    I'VE KILLED THE ONLY WOMAN I LOVED
              A   E   A
    BECAUSE SHE WOULD NOT BE MY BRIDE

    CHORUS

LESSON 5
TRAVIS PICKING, CONTINUED

For a second Travis picking pattern, we're going to reverse the order in which we pick the upper strings with our index and middle fingers. Start on a C7 chord this time, just the bass notes on the fifth and fourth strings (Example 1). Next, add in your middle finger on the second string, just after each *lower* bass note on the fifth string (Example 2). When you've got that going smoothly, add in your index finger on the third string, just after each *upper* bass note on the fourth string (Example 3).

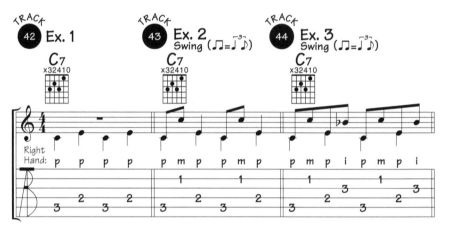

Notice that these examples are being played with a swing-eighth-note feel, instead of the straight-eighth-note feel we used in the last lesson. Example 4 is a side-by-side comparison of this pattern played with a straight feel and with a swing feel.

To play this pattern on a G chord, keep your index finger on the third string and your middle finger on the second string, and alternate your thumb between the sixth string and the fourth string, as in Example 5.

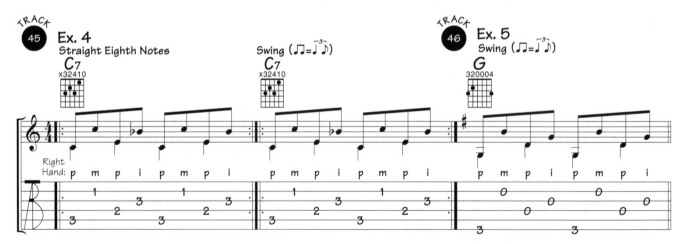

As we discussed in the last lesson, fingerpicking allows you to use certain chord voicings that might not work with strumming, because you can pick out just the notes you want. By taking a C7 chord and moving it up two frets, we can get a new kind of D7 chord.

To Travis-pick on this chord, we stick to the same pattern, using just the middle four strings and avoiding the first and sixth strings, which don't really fit. Example 6 shows the pattern on this D7 chord. We've got one new note here, an F♯ at the fourth fret of the fourth string (an octave higher than the F♯ on the sixth string we played in the last lesson). Note also that this D7 includes a D bass note at the fifth fret of the fifth string; up until now, we've been playing this same note on the open fourth string. And there's a C note at the fifth fret of the third string—we've been playing this same note on the first fret of the second string. Playing notes at a different *position,* or location, on the fingerboard enables us to create a different sound.

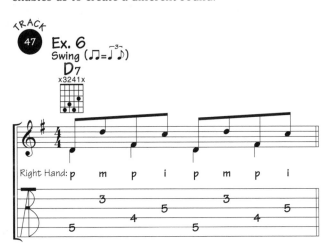

SMOOTH MOVES

With this D7, you just have to slide your whole hand up two frets to get from C7 to D7, and slide it back to return to C7. Getting from D7 back to G is a little trickier, though, since you have to jump back two frets *and* change fingerings. Here's one practice idea that may help: when you go from D7 to G, you can move your middle and ring fingers together, from the bottom two notes of D7 to the bottom two notes of G.

You can practice this move without even playing the chords, just moving your fretting hand back and forth. Then try to make the change from a full D7 to a full G. It's natural to lift off from the full D7, grab just those bottom two notes of the G first, and then get your pinky into place after that. That actually works, because it gets the bass notes in place right away, and you're not even picking the high string with this particular pattern.

To practice the picking, go back and forth between D7 and G playing just the relevant bass notes with your thumb, as in Example 7. In Example 8, add in the notes played with your middle finger just after each low bass note, and your index finger after each higher bass note.

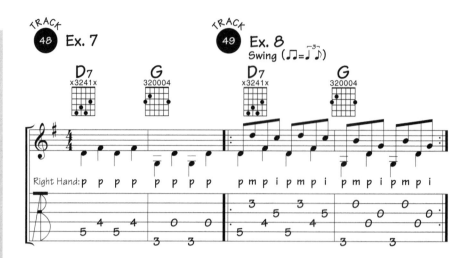

Let's take this new pattern, with the swing feel and our new D7 chord, and play "Crawdad," also known variously as "Crawdad Hole" and "The Crawdad Song."

CRAWDAD

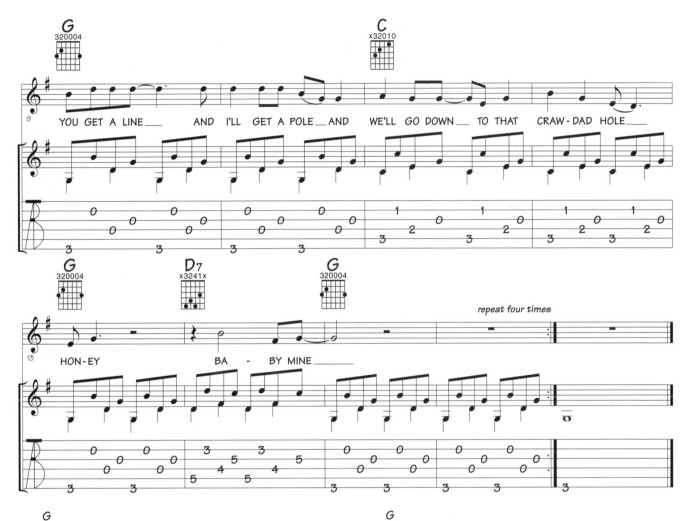

1. G
YOU GET A LINE AND I'LL GET A POLE, HONEY
                              D7
YOU GET A LINE AND I'LL GET A POLE, BABE
G
YOU GET A LINE AND I'LL GET A POLE
      C
AND WE'LL GO DOWN TO THE CRAWDAD HOLE
G   D7   G
HONEY, BABY, MINE

2. G
ALONG COME A MAN WITH A SACK ON HIS BACK, HONEY
                                   D7
ALONG COME A MAN WITH A SACK ON HIS BACK, BABE
G
ALONG COME A MAN WITH A SACK ON HIS BACK
C
HE'S GOT MORE CRAWDADS THAN HE CAN PACK
G   D7   G
HONEY, BABY, MINE

3. G
WHAT YOU GONNA DO WHEN THE LAKE GOES DRY, HONEY
                              D7
WHAT YOU GONNA DO WHEN THE LAKE GOES DRY, BABE
G
WHAT YOU GONNA DO WHEN THE LAKE GOES DRY
C
SIT ON THE BANK AND WATCH THE CRAWDADS DIE
G   D7   G
HONEY, BABY, MINE

4. G
NOW, WHAT YOU GONNA DO WHEN THE CRAWDADS DIE, HONEY
                                   D7
WHAT YOU GONNA DO WHEN THE CRAWDADS DIE, BABE
G
WHAT YOU GONNA DO WHEN THE CRAWDADS DIE
C
SIT ON THE BANK UNTIL I CRY
G   D7   G
HONEY, BABY, MINE

5. G
WHAT DID THE HEN-DUCK SAY TO THE DRAKE, HONEY
                              D7
WHAT DID THE HEN-DUCK SAY TO THE DRAKE, BABE
G
WHAT DID THE HEN-DUCK SAY TO THE DRAKE
            C
WELL THERE AIN'T NO CRAWDADS IN THIS LAKE
G   D7   G
HONEY, BABY, MINE

LESSON 6
HAMMER-ONS

By now you may be listening to some recordings of guitarists playing fiddle tunes and other melodies, and you may have found yourself thinking, "Hey now, wait a minute. I can play that melody, and it doesn't sound like *that*. How do they get it to sound so smooth?"

Well, here is one of the secrets: the *hammer-on*. A hammer-on is when you pick a note and then hammer a finger down at a higher fret on the same string, sounding a second note without picking the string again. Listen to the difference in Example 1: the first time, both notes are picked; the second time, the first note is picked and the second note is hammered on, creating a smoother transition between the notes. As you can see, a hammer-on is indicated with a connecting line between the two notes, called a *slur,* plus an *H* above the tab.

So try it. In Example 2, play the open G string, then drop your second finger onto the fingerboard at the second fret to sound the note A.

In Example 3, try doing a handful of hammer-ons in a row. Then in Example 4, try switching back and forth between hammer-ons on two different strings.

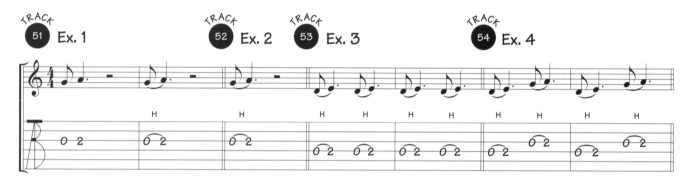

HAMMER IT!

Here's the most important thing to remember in getting the second note to sound: this is called a *hammer-on*, not a *press-on*. If you pick the first note and then slowly press your finger into the string, you're going to kill the string's vibration before it actually makes contact with the second fret. You'll hear your first note and then a depressing little *phththt* sound where your second note was supposed to happen. Drop your finger to the fretboard with conviction! Bring it down in a single quick gesture and aim for the fretboard, not the string—think of the string as something getting crushed on your way to the wood below.

Example 5 combines hammer-ons with regular picked notes on the same string, while Example 6 combines hammer-ons with regular picked notes on an adjacent string. Finally, Example 7 is a short run in the key of C that works as a cool ending phrase.

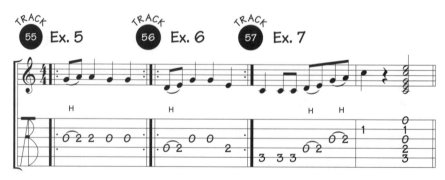

Let's see how this works when you're playing an actual tune. At right is the melody to "New River Train" in C. If you want to play the accompaniment part on the CD, the pattern is shown in Example 8.

NEW RIVER TRAIN

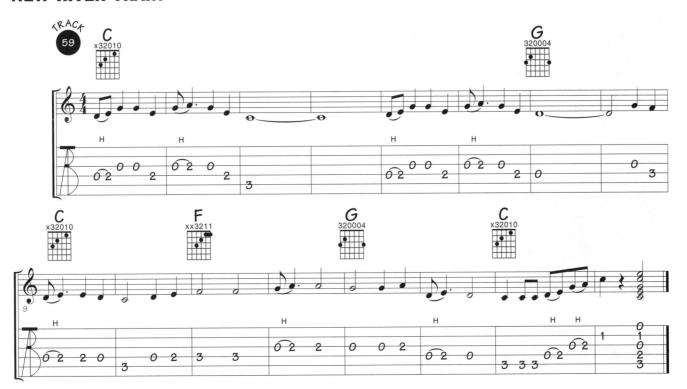

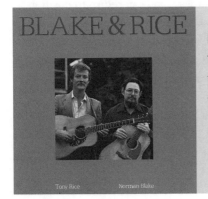

ESSENTIAL LISTENING

The front-porch atmosphere of much of **Norman Blake**'s solo work comfortably cloaks the fact that you're dealing with a first-class composer, dedicated tune researcher, and highly respected session musician as well as a top-notch flatpicker and singer. He and newgrasser **Tony Rice** prove perfect foils for one another on their duet album *Blake and Rice* (Rounder), which includes their version of **"New River Train."** For an early Bill Monroe version (before he started the Blue Grass Boys), check out *The Essential Bill Monroe and the Monroe Brothers* (RCA). From 1967 there's Doc Watson's *Old Timey Concert* (Vanguard), and for a recent yet old-timey take, try Mike Seeger and Paul Brown's *Way Down in North Carolina* (Rounder).

LESSON 7
SLIDES AND PULL-OFFS

Now that you've added those slick-sounding hammer-ons to your bag of tricks, let's turn to two other essential techniques for spicing up a melody: *slides* and *pull-offs.*

A slide is when you pick a fretted note and then slide your finger up or down the string to another fret, sounding another note. We're going to focus on sliding to a higher note, usually a fret or two up from the starting note. In Example 1, listen to the difference between a hammer-on from the second to the fourth fret of the G string, and a slide between the same two notes. The slide is indicated with a slur and an angled line between the two notes and an *S* above the tab.

TRACK **60** Ex. 1

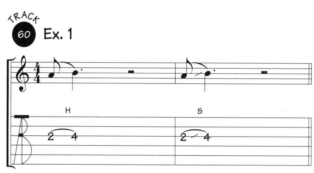

Here's how the slide works: pick the first note, then, keeping your finger pressed to the fingerboard the whole time, move it along the string until you're at the fourth fret. Moving in a single quick, decisive gesture is as important here as it is for hammering on. If you move slowly, or let up the pressure at any point along the way, you'll stop the string's vibrations and never hear the second note. So imagine that your finger is really sliding up the *fingerboard,* pressed to the wood, with the string caught in between.

The thumb stays anchored while the finger slides up.

Note: You don't want to move your whole hand up the neck as you slide, nor do you want to push just that one finger up the fingerboard, stretching it out and losing its arch. The ideal movement is one where your thumb serves as an anchor on the side of the neck closest to you and the fingers of your hand pivot up together on the far side of the neck. That way, you can return to position by just pivoting your fingers back into alignment with your thumb.

Try doing a series of slides on the third string, as in Example 2. Notice that we're sliding up to a B note. Until now we've played B on the open second string, but since B is a whole step (two frets) up from A, there is also a B at the fourth fret of the third string.

One very common slide move is to make this slide from A to B and then play the open B note afterward, as in Example 3. When that feels comfortable, try Example 4, in which you follow the slide move in Example 3 with some regular fretted notes.

Another useful move is to slide from F♯ to G on the fourth string and then play an open G on the third string. G is a half step up from F♯, so we can find a new G at the fifth fret of the fourth string, just above the fourth-fret F♯. This move, shown in Example 5, is the basis for one of the all-time classic *kick-offs* or introductions in country and bluegrass. Try it in Example 6.

If we go up a whole step from the D at the third fret on the second string, we'll get an E at the fifth fret. Example 7 shows another useful move: slide from D to E on the second string and then play an open E on the high string.

PULL-OFFS

Hammer-ons and the types of slides we've been learning take you from a lower note to a higher note. A pull-off takes you from a higher note to a lower one: you play a fretted note and then pull your finger off of the string, sounding a second note without making a second pick (or finger) stroke. In Example 8, listen to the difference between picking both a G and an E on the first string, and pulling off from a G to an E. The pull-off is indicated by a slur between the two notes and a *P* above the tab.

The important thing about a pull-off is that it means literally pulling at the string as you remove your finger. If you pick the first note and then just lift your finger straight up in the air, you won't get the full sound of the second note. So try this: pick the first note, then pull your finger down toward the floor to remove it from the string. Keep your finger pressed against the fretboard as you go. You're basically plucking the string with your fretting finger as you leave the first note. In Example 9, try it on the high string.

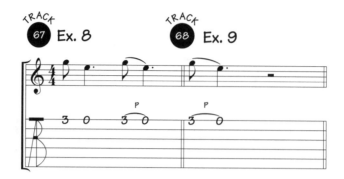

When you do a pull-off on one of the lower strings, the trick is to avoid creating too much noise on the strings next to the one you're pulling off. Try Example 10, a pull-off on the third string. As you pull off of the first note (A at the second fret), pull toward the floor but try to minimize how far your finger travels after you release the string. In time, you will get to where you hear the second note as loudly as the first without hitting any of the other strings. Example 11 is an exercise for playing pull-offs in between regular picked notes.

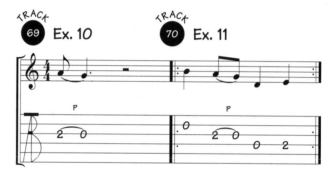

Now let's revisit "Sail Away Ladies," which we learned in Book 2, and play it using slides on the third and second strings and pull-offs on the third and first strings. Notice the hammer-ons, too, in measures 14 and 22.

SAIL AWAY LADIES

LESSON 8
ALTERNATE BASS NOTES

Let's get back to strum patterns with an alternating bass, but this time we will play some different bass notes to fill out and vary the sound.

On a chord like D, which is played on just the top four strings, you can really fill out the sound by going below the root (the open fourth string) to the fifth string for your second bass note. Ordinarily, we'd alternate between the fourth and the third string, as in Example 1. Now we're talking about doing an alternating bass that sounds like Example 2.

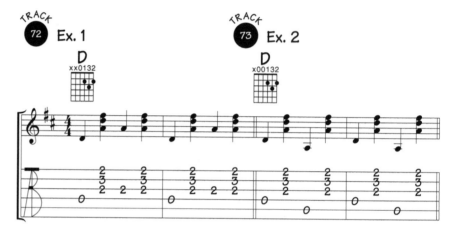

If this is a bit elusive at first, try breaking it down. First, get just the two bass strings going (Example 3). Next, play the first bass note, follow it with a strum, and then hit the bass note on the fifth string (Example 4).

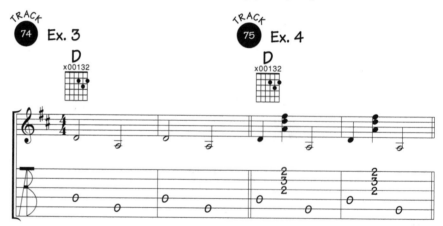

Now if you add in the strum after the second bass note, you'll be playing the full pattern of Example 2. You can use the same pattern on D7 and D minor as well.

On A major (as well as A7 or A minor), you can do the same kind of thing, starting with a bass note on the fifth string and using the sixth string for the second bass note, as in Example 5.

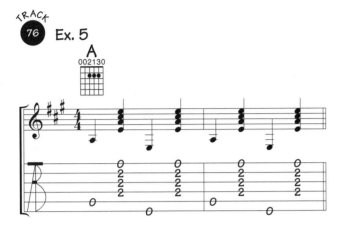

SWITCHING PATTERNS

If you have a chord progression that includes some kind of D chord with this new pattern, along with, say, a C chord using a regular bass/strum pattern where the second bass note is higher than the first bass note, it can take a bit of practice to coordinate everything. Try Example 6, where you switch between a measure of D minor and a measure of C major.

The same thing happens if you switch from some kind of A chord with this new bass pattern to a chord like G, on which you can only play our original bass/strum pattern. Try alternating between a measure of A minor with the new pattern and a measure of G with the original pattern, as in Example 7.

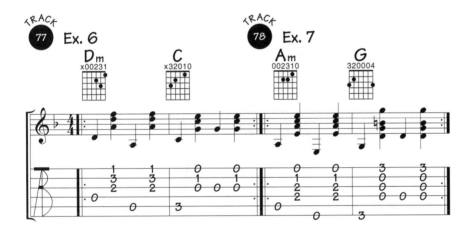

We're now ready for our next song. "Little Sadie," you will see, has something a little weird going on in measure 11—the G chord lasts for two extra beats. So the time signature switches temporarily to 6/4, which means six quarter notes in a measure rather than the usual four. We'll be using the original bass/strum pattern with the lower bass note first, so with two extra beats, you'll actually play the pattern shown in measure 11: the low bass note, a strum, the upper bass note, a strum, and then another low bass note and a strum. Then you move onto the next chord.

Now here's "Little Sadie," with the new bass/strum pattern on all the D minors and A minors and the original pattern on the C's and G's. Notice also the hammer-on with the Dm chord. If you play the Dm with the fingering shown (middle, pinky, index), you can reach over and grab that hammer on the fifth string with your ring finger while still holding the chord position. Try it, but if this move is giving you too much trouble, stick with the Dm bass/strum we practiced in Example 6.

LITTLE SADIE

1.
    Dm
WENT OUT LAST NIGHT FOR TO MAKE A LITTLE ROUND
  C   **Am**
I MET LITTLE SADIE AND I SHOT HER DOWN

WENT BACK HOME, GOT INTO BED
G   **Dm**
FORTY-FOUR PISTOL UNDER MY HEAD

2.
    Dm
WOKE UP THE NEXT MORNING 'BOUT HALF PAST NINE
  C   **Am**
THE HACKS AND THE BUGGIES ALL STANDING IN LINE

GENTS AND THE GAMBLERS ALL STANDING 'ROUND
  G   **Dm**
TO CARRY LITTLE SADIE TO HER BURYING GROUND

3.
    Dm
THEN I BEGAN TO THINK ABOUT THE DEED I'D DONE
  C   **Am**
I GRABBED MY HAT AND AWAY I RUN

I MADE A GOOD RUN, BUT A LITTLE TOO SLOW
    G   **Dm**
THEY OVERTOOK ME IN JERICHO

4.
    Dm
I WAS STANDING ON THE CORNER, READING THE BILL
   C   **Am**
WHEN UP STEPPED THE SHERIFF OF THOMASVILLE

HE SAID "YOUNG MAN IF YOUR NAME'S BROWN
  G   **Dm**
REMEMBER THE NIGHT YOU SHOT SADIE DOWN"

5.
    Dm
WELL I SAID "YES SIR BUT MY NAME IS LEE
  C   **Am**
I MURDERED LITTLE SADIE IN THE FIRST DEGREE

FIRST DEGREE AND THE SECOND DEGREE
  G   **Dm**
YOU GOT ANY PAPERS WON'T YOU READ THEM TO ME"

6.
    Dm
THEY TOOK ME DOWNTOWN, DRESSED ME IN BLACK
C   **Am**
PUT ME ON THE TRAIN AND STARTED ME BACK

ALL THE WAY BACK TO THAT THOMASVILLE JAIL
  G   **Dm**
AND I HAD NO MONEY FOR TO GO MY BAIL

7.
    Dm
THE JUDGE AND JURY TOOK THEIR STAND
  C   **Am**
THE JUDGE HAD THE PAPERS IN HIS RIGHT HAND

FORTY-ONE DAYS AND FORTY-ONE NIGHTS
G   **Dm**
FORTY-ONE YEARS TO WEAR THE BALL AND STRIPES

ESSENTIAL LISTENING

Tony Rice recorded **"Little Sadie"** on his third solo release, *Manzanita* (Rounder), with a no-slouches crew that included Dobroist Jerry Douglas and mandolinists Sam Bush, Ricky Skaggs, and David Grisman. Rice's version drew at least in part on Doc Watson's 1964 version on *Doc Watson and Son* (Vanguard). More recently, new old-timers the Freight Hoppers included "Little Sadie" on *Where'd You Come From, Where'd You Go* (Rounder), and **Tim O'Brien and Darrell Scott** laid down a version on their collection of living-room duets, *Real Time* (Howdy Skies).

LESSON 9
THE PINCH

Let's get back to Travis-style fingerpicking and build on our original pattern with a new technique called a *pinch,* which involves playing two notes at the same time, one with your thumb and one with your finger.

We'll start with an A-minor chord, using the pattern where your middle finger follows the first bass note and your index finger follows the second bass note, as in Example 1.

Now let's add in a pinch: in Example 2, you play the bass note and the second-string A minor at the same time. Then in Example 3, replace the first two eighth notes of the pattern in Example 1 with the pinch in Example 2. The pinch lasts for a quarter note, so it takes up the same amount of time as those two eighth notes did. Watch the counting carefully and, in Example 3, continue on with the pattern in beats 2, 3, and 4 after making the pinch on beat 1.

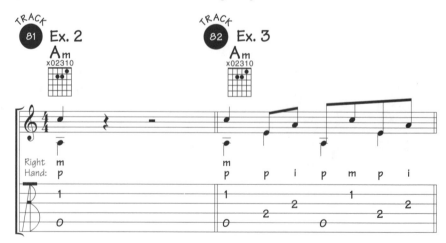

From your lofty perch here at the end of Book 3, you hardly need me to tell you what comes next: practice playing this new pattern in a loop, starting slowly and evenly and only bringing it up to speed when you can do so without dropping any beats or losing your place.

Once you've got all this happening over A minor, it's time to take on another chord using the same pattern. Example 4 shows how it'll work on a G chord. Once again, old pro that you are now, you know what comes next: practice keeping the pattern going while you switch between A minor and G. If you find that tricky at first, try Examples 5 and 6. In Example 5, you play a bar of A minor with

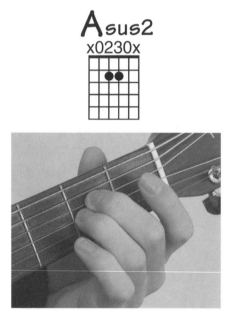

the pattern, followed by just the first pinch on the G chord. Example 6 is the flip side: play a measure of G with the pattern, landing on just the first pinch of the A minor.

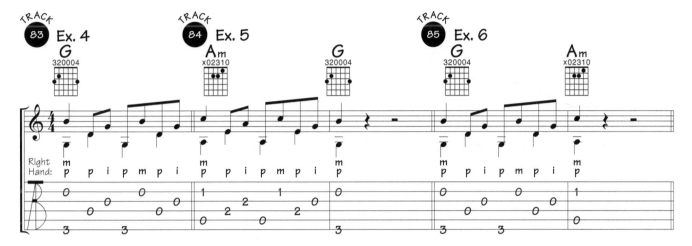

Let's dress up the A minor a bit. First, take off your index finger, creating something with the sophisticated-sounding name of Asus2 (see chord grid and photo on page 124).

Next, in Example 7, start with an A-minor chord, then lift your index finger off for beats 3 and 4. Since the pinch emphasizes the top note of the picking pattern, right on the downbeat, you can create a little melody within the pattern just by changing that top note around.

Let's take this idea one step further. Starting on the Asus2 chord, do the pinch and then hammer on with your index finger to form the full A-minor chord, as in Example 8. Now use this hammer-on to start what is otherwise just a regular bar of A minor, as in Example 9. Your right hand plays exactly the same pattern as before.

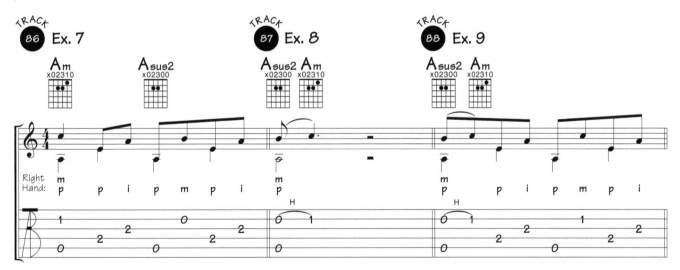

To put these moves into action, let's play "Omie Wise," yet another fine traditional ballad fraught with greed, lust, betrayal, and other messy details of love gone wrong. The introduction is a four-bar vamp in which you alternate between A minor and Asus2 (measures 1, 3) and play a hammer-on into a full measure of A minor (measures 2, 4). These moves also occur during the song itself, in measures 5–6, 9–10, and 12–13.

OMIE WISE

```
        Am       Asus2 Am         G
1.  OH LISTEN TO MY STORY I'LL TELL YOU NO LIES
        Am       Asus2  Am        G              Am Asus2
    HOW JOHN LEWIS DID MURDER POOR LITTLE OMIE WISE

        Am       Asus2 Am          G
2.  HE TOLD HER TO MEET HIM AT ADAMS' SPRING
          Am Asus2 Am            G           Am Asus2
    HE PROMISED HER MONEY AND OTHER FINE THINGS

          Am       Asus2    Am         G
3.  SO LIKE A FOOL SHE MET HIM AT ADAMS' SPRING
          Am      Asus2 Am         G        Am Asus2
    NO MONEY DID HE BRING HER, NOR OTHER FINE THINGS

           Am        Asus2 Am        G
4.  "GO WITH ME LITTLE OMIE AND AWAY WE WILL GO
          Am Asus2 Am          G           Am Asus2
    WE'LL GO AND GET MARRIED AND NO ONE WILL KNOW"

           Am       Asus2 Am          G
5.  SHE CLIMBED UP BEHIND HIM AND AWAY THEY DID GO
    Am   Asus2 Am         G           Am Asus2
    OFF TO THE RIVER WHERE DEEP WATERS FLOW

        Am Asus2     Am            G
6.  "JOHN LEWIS, JOHN LEWIS, WILL YOU TELL ME YOUR MIND
        Am        Asus2 Am        G          Am Asus2
    DO YOU INTEND TO MARRY ME OR LEAVE ME BEHIND"

           Am       Asus2 Am       G
7.  "LITTLE OMIE, LITTLE OMIE, I'LL TELL YOU MY MIND
        Am    Asus2 Am          G          Am Asus2
    MY MIND IS TO DROWN YOU AND LEAVE YOU BEHIND"

           Am       Asus2 Am       G
8.  "HAVE MERCY ON MY BABY AND SPARE ME MY LIFE
        Am       Asus2 Am         G        Am Asus2
    I'LL GO HOME AS A BEGGAR AND NEVER BE YOUR WIFE"

           Am       Asus2 Am         G
9.  HE KISSED HER AND HUGGED HER AND TURNED HER AROUND
           Am           Asus2 Am
    THEN PUSHED HER IN DEEP WATERS WHERE HE
        G            Am Asus2
    KNEW SHE WOULD DROWN
```

```
        Am   Asus2 Am         G
10. HE GOT ON HIS PONY AND AWAY HE DID RIDE
           Am           Asus2 Am
    AS THE SCREAMS OF LITTLE OMIE
             G              Am Asus2
    WENT DOWN BY HIS SIDE

           Am       Asus2   Am
11. IT WAS ON A THURSDAY MORNING, AND THE
        G
    RAIN WAS POURING DOWN
              Am       Asus2       Am
    WHEN THE PEOPLE SEARCHED FOR OMIE
          G              Am Asus2
    BUT SHE COULD NOT BE FOUND

          Am       Asus2  Am          G
12. THEN TWO BOYS WENT A-FISHIN' ONE FINE SUMMER DAY
          Am         Asus2 Am    G       Am Asus2
    AND SAW LITTLE OMIE'S BODY GO FLOATING AWAY

          Am          Asus2 Am
13. THEY THREW THEIR NET AROUND HER
          G
    AND DREW HER TO THE BANK
        Am          Asus2 Am
    HER CLOTHES ALL WET AND MUDDY
          G              Am Asus2
    THEY LAID HER ON A PLANK

          Am   Asus2   Am         G
14. THEY SENT FOR JOHN LEWIS TO COME TO THAT PLACE
          Am          Asus2 Am
    AND BROUGHT HER OUT BEFORE HIM
             G                Am Asus2
    SO THAT HE MIGHT SEE HER FACE

          Am   Asus2 Am              G
15. HE MADE NO CONFESSION BUT THEY CARRIED HIM TO JAIL
          Am       Asus2 Am         G        Am Asus2
    NO FRIENDS NOR RELATIONS WOULD GO ON HIS BAIL
```

ESSENTIAL LISTENING

Like the Texas songster Mance Lipscomb, Kentucky banjoist and singer **Roscoe Holcomb** wasn't recorded until his discovery during the folk revival. His version of the classic murder ballad **"Omie Wise"** appears on *The High Lonesome Sound* (Smithsonian Folkways). For a prewar take, check out the duo of fiddler G.B. Grayson and guitarist Henry Whitter on *The Recordings of Grayson and Whitter: 1928–1930* (County). From 1964, there's Doc Watson's version on his first Vanguard release, *Doc Watson,* and from across the water, check out Bert Jansch and John Renbourn's mesmerizing twin fingerpicking arrangement of the tune on *A Maid That's Deep in Love* (Shanachie).

LESSON 10
ALL TOGETHER NOW

For our Book 3 finale, let's put several of our new ideas together and wrap up with an extremely cool song, "That'll Never Happen No More."

We used a Travis-picking pattern with a swing feel in Lesson 5 to play "Crawdad." Now we'll combine elements of Lesson 1 (swing eighth notes) and Lesson 3 (playing two chords per measure) with a variation on Lesson 5's Travis-picking pattern to play this classic ragtime piece.

We've already worked on the switch between a G chord and the D7 played up at the third fret position. Example 1 shows a common way to make this change a little easier when you're playing more up-tempo material: drop off the last note of the D7 measure before returning to G. If you left out that last note on every measure, it would give things too much of a stop-and-start feeling. At the end of every other measure, however, it not only makes it easier to return to the G, it opens up a little breathing room in the music.

Now try this idea on another pair of chords: G and E7. You can pick the same strings for E7 as you do for G, so just keep the pattern going with your right hand when you change chords with your left (Example 2).

A7 can be picked using the same strings as D7; try using our two-bar pattern on these two chords as well (Example 3).

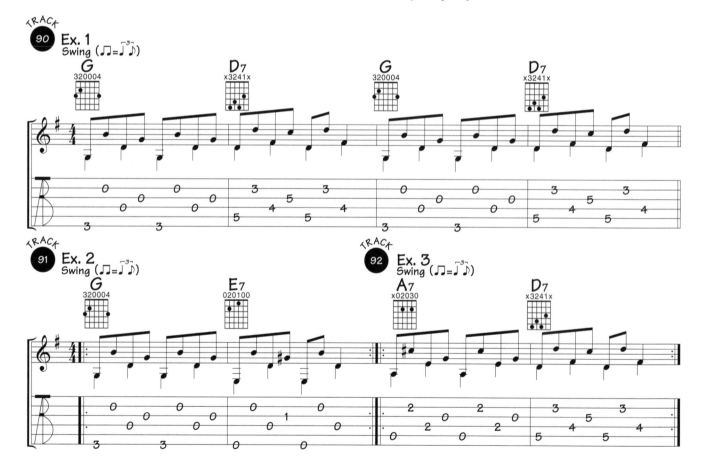

In Lesson 3 we looked at how to split a bass/strum pattern over two chords in one measure; now we'll see how to do that with a Travis-picking pattern. To play a split measure of A7 and D7, or two beats of A7 and two beats of D7, your right hand doesn't have to do anything new. Just play a full measure of the picking pattern. Start by fingering an A7 chord, and as you make the change to D7 with your left hand after two beats, just keep motoring on with your right-hand thumb and fingers as if nothing had happened. Try this in Example 4, which leaves off the last note of the pattern on the D7.

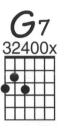

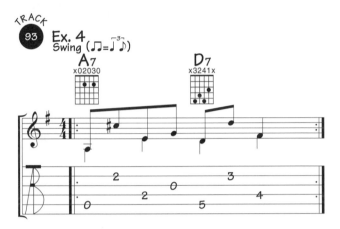

"That'll Never Happen No More" has an instrumental section between verses that includes a couple of chords we haven't seen before. First look at the new, abbreviated form of G7, with the pinky moved over to the fourth string. Practice switching between G and G7 in Example 5.

Now try the E♭7, which is just like the D7 chord we've been using but moved up one fret. In Example 6, try switching from a C chord up to an E♭7 and back.

DOIN' THAT RAG

When all of these moves feel comfortable, you're ready to tackle "That'll Never Happen No More" on page 130. The song has a verse, a chorus, and an instrumental section. The chorus includes a short instrumental tag after the last words are sung, and we'll use this tag for our introduction too. For an ending, use the instrumental section (measures 13–24).

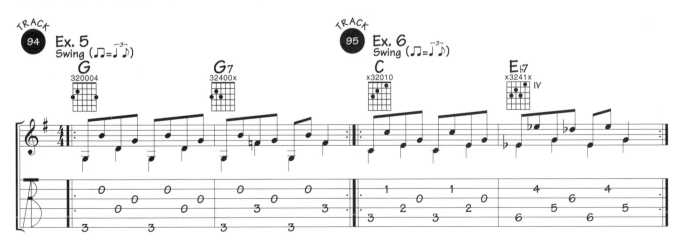

THAT'LL NEVER HAPPEN NO MORE

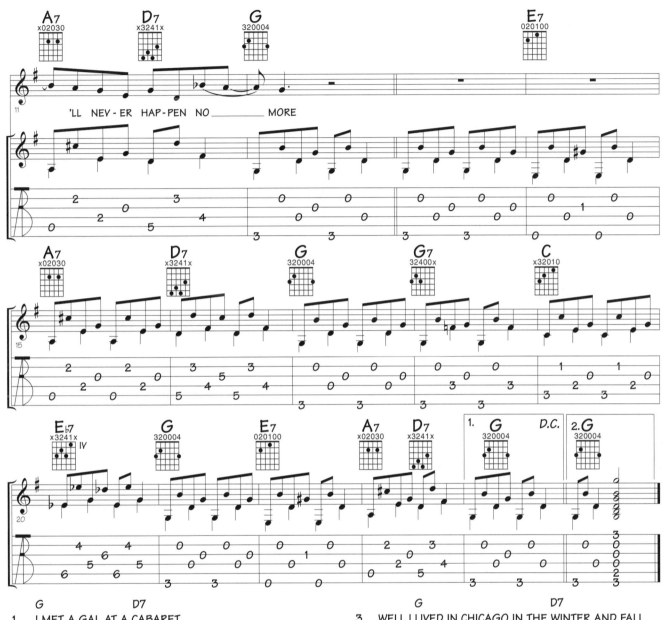

'LL NEV-ER HAP-PEN NO _____ MORE

G   D7
1. I MET A GAL AT A CABARET
    G   D7
    SAID "PRETTY PAPA YOU GOIN' MY WAY?"
    G   D7
    I GUESS YOU KNOW WHAT IT'S ALL ABOUT
              A7   D7
    SHE TOOK ME HOME JUST TO KICK ME OUT

    G   D7
2. BROKE MY NOSE AND SHE SPLIT MY CHIN
    G   D7
    "DON'T LET ME CATCH YOU 'ROUND HERE AGAIN"
    G   D7
    CHASED ME THROUGH THE KITCHEN, OUT THROUGH THE DOOR
              A7   D7
    SHE BEAT ME WITH A CHAIR TILL MY HEAD GOT SORE

         G   E7
    BUT THAT'LL NEVER HAPPEN NO MORE
    A7   D7   G
    THAT'LL NEVER HAPPEN NO MORE
    G   E7   A7 D7
    G   G7   C Eb7
    G   E7   A7 D7 G

G   D7
3. WELL I LIVED IN CHICAGO IN THE WINTER AND FALL
    G   D7
    IT TAUGHT ME TO WEAR MY OVERALLS
    G   D7
    I GOT BROKE, AND IT WAS MY FAULT
         A7   D7
    I WAS USED TO EATING PORK CHOPS WITH A WHOLE LOT OF SALT

    G   D7
4. I MET A GAL IN A BIG MINK COAT
    G   D7
    FANCY CAR AND A FORTY-FOOT BOAT
    G   D7
    SHE PULLED A GUN, YOU KNOW SHE TOOK MY DOUGH
         A7   D7
    I DIDN'T HOLLER AND I DIDN'T SAY NO, I SAID

         CHORUS

CONGRATULATIONS

Well, all right! You've made it through all three books of *The Acoustic Guitar Method*. Think about how much we've covered: We started with just a few chords and basic strums, worked on switching between chords, began some note reading, and learned notes on the fingerboard. From there, we got into playing bass/strum patterns and more chords, single notes, and complete melodies. With those tools together, we moved into more complete alternating-bass strums over all different kinds of songs, began to incorporate bass runs, and learned about fingerpicking patterns. Finally, we built on all of that by learning about swing-eighth rhythms, Travis-picking patterns, hammer-ons, pull-offs, and slides. And along the way, we learned more than 30 great songs.

So what's next? Well, first, as you may have already realized, you could apply much of what we've learned in later lessons to the songs we first saw in Book 1 and the beginning of Book 2. Try "In the Pines" with the 3/4 picking pattern from "House of the Rising Sun," or use an alternating-bass strum with bass runs on "Hot Corn, Cold Corn." See what the swing-eighths pattern from "Delia" sounds like on "Alberta." Experiment.

Second, if you've been checking out any of the suggested recordings, you've probably heard at least a few songs that grab your ear. See if you can hear what the chords are, get a songbook with the words and chords written out, or ask another guitar player or your teacher to show you the basic parts of the song. Then try working out the bass/strum patterns and bass runs for the song, or, if it sounds more appropriate, try one or more of the different fingerpicking patterns we've learned.

Above all, play and sing the songs you like best, practice the hard parts slowly and carefully, listen to great music—whatever that means to *you*—for inspiration, and remember to have fun. Good luck.

ESSENTIAL LISTENING: THE SHORT LIST

There have been many recordings recommended throughout these books. If you're feeling somewhat overwhelmed, or you just want to have a little left over for new strings when you leave the CD store, here are five to start with.

Anthology of American Folk Music (Smithsonian Folkways). Also known informally as the Harry Smith collection, this three-CD collection was originally issued in 1952 on LP and provides a cross-section of blues, hillbilly, Cajun, and gospel music recorded in the late 1920s and early 1930s. Even with digital remastering, it's not for the faint-hearted—the music can be pretty raw, and the sound quality is often rough too. There's an equal balance of well-known and obscure artists represented, and it's particularly interesting to sort through these tracks in light of the impact it had on the folk revival of the '50s and '60s.

Folkways: The Original Vision (Smithsonian Folkways). Woody Guthrie and Leadbelly are both extensively documented on Folkways and elsewhere playing both traditional and original material; this single disc offers a succinct sampler of some of the better-known songs they wrote.

Doc Watson, *The Best of Doc Watson: 1964–1968* (Vanguard). An excellent overview of Watson's highly influential repertoire and approach as they crystallized in the mid-'60s. Most cuts find Watson playing solo or with just second guitar and/or bass for backup, as he sings, flatpicks, and fingerpicks everything from country songs and traditional ballads to blues tunes and signature instrumentals like "Black Mountain Rag" and "Windy and Warm."

Bill Monroe, *The Father of Bluegrass* (Living Era). A good one-CD look at the genesis of Monroe's music and consequently of bluegrass itself, starting with recordings by the earliest incarnations of the Blue Grass Boys and concluding with ten tracks by the classic mid-'40s lineup that included Lester Flatt and Earl Scruggs. For a more in-depth collection, the four-CD *Music of Bill Monroe* (MCA) spans Monroe's entire recording career and includes dozens of now-standard songs and instrumentals performed by a who's who of bluegrass musicians.

Mississippi John Hurt, *Avalon Blues: The Complete 1928 Recordings* (Columbia/Legacy). Countless folk and blues guitarists and folk-influenced songwriters trace their lineage back to John Hurt's elegant, rolling fingerpicking style. And his singing makes it clear that you don't have to holler to sing the blues. These 13 tunes are the only recordings Hurt had made prior to his rediscovery in the 1960s.

CHORDS CAPOED UP THE NECK

No capo	Capo fret 1	2	3	4	5	6	7
A	A♯/B♭	B	C	C♯/D♭	D	D♯/E♭	E
C	C♯/D♭	D	D♯/E♭	E	F	F♯/G♭	G
D	D♯/E♭	E	F	F♯/G♭	G	G♯/A♭	A
E	F	F♯/G♭	G	G♯/A♭	A	A♯/B♭	B
G	G♯/A♭	A	A♯/B♭	B	C	C♯/D♭	D

ABOUT THE AUTHOR

David Hamburger is a performer and writer who lives in Austin, Texas. He has been playing folk and blues music since first picking up the guitar at the age of 12 and has been on the faculty of the National Guitar Workshop since 1988. Hamburger's guitar, slide guitar, and Dobro playing can be heard on his solo albums *King of the Brooklyn Delta* (Chester, 1994) and *Indigo Rose* (Chester, 1999), as well as on numerous other independent recordings.

Hamburger is the author of four other books, including *Acoustic Guitar Slide Basics,* and has contributed dozens of lessons and articles to *Guitar Player* and *Acoustic Guitar* magazines. For a discography, performance schedule, and other information, visit his Web site at www.davidhamburger.com.

ACKNOWLEDGMENTS

Thanks to Jeffrey Pepper Rodgers for his detailed and patient editing; Andrew DuBrock for his equally careful attention to the music itself; David Lusterman for hatching this scheme in the first place; the String Letter staff for all their various efforts, past, present, and future; Carl Thiel at Carl Thiel Music; Bradley Kopp at The Ranch; Wayne Rooks; and Guadalupe Arts. Special thanks to Catherine Berry, who thinks that writing books is really cool. And to Lucille Magliozzi, wherever you are: all the things you taught me are in these pages somewhere.

ABOUT STRING LETTER PUBLISHING

String Letter Publishing, which was founded in 1986, is the source for acoustic music magazines and books. We serve musicians, aficionados, and listeners with news, information, advice, and entertainment through a wide selection of products. Our specialty is music where songs and stringed instruments play a major role: roots, jazz, blues, rock, classical, and other traditional and contemporary styles. From songbooks to guidebooks to pictorial reference works, String Letter books are enduring resources for acoustic musicians and students who want to improve their playing skills, expand their musical horizons, and become more knowledgeable about instruments and gear. Learn more at www.stringletter.com.

String Letter publishes *Acoustic Guitar,* the magazine for all acoustic guitar players, from beginners to performing professionals. Through interviews, reviews, workshops, sheet music, and song transcriptions, *Acoustic Guitar* readers learn music from around the globe and get to know the artists who create it. With product reviews and expert advice, *Acoustic Guitar* also helps readers become smarter buyers and owners of acoustic guitars and guitar gear. For more information, visit us on the Web at www.acousticguitar.com.

Certificate of Completion

This certifies that

_____

has mastered *The Acoustic Guitar Method.*

Teacher _____

Date _____

Hal Leonard Presents Guitar Instruction from

S T R I N G   L E T T E R   P U B L I S H I N G

ACOUSTIC GUITAR BASICS

ACCOMPANIMENT BASICS

This book and CD by the master teachers at *Acoustic Guitar* magazine will give both beginners and seasoned players the essentials of acoustic guitar accompaniment. Fingerpicking and flatpicking techniques are employed in a number of roots styles including folk, rock, blues, Celtic and bluegrass.

_____00695430 Book/CD Pack..........................$14.95

CHORD AND HARMONY BASICS

by Dylan Schorer

Whether you're a beginning or an intermediate acoustic guitarist, chords are the foundation for the songs you play. This book teaches you the real-world chord voicings, shapes and progressions used by today's top acoustic players. Not a chord encyclopedia, *Acoustic Guitar Chord and Harmony Basics* shows you what you really need to know, and offers valuable tips and tricks to help you understand and master the sounds of bluegrass, blues, folk, rock and roots music.

_____00695611 Book/CD Pack..........................$16.95

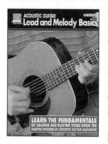

LEAD AND MELODY BASICS

This book introduces students to the essentials of playing melodies and leads in a number of roots styles, including folk, blues, Celtic and bluegrass. Includes a full lineup of lessons and 9 songs (including Cripple Creek • Pink Panther Theme • Arkansas Traveler) expertly played – slowly & up to tempo – by the teachers on the accompanying CD.

_____00695492 Book/CD Pack..........................$14.95

RHYTHM BASICS

by Dylan Schorer

Strong, tight rhythm is essential to your success as a guitarist, *Acoustic Guitar Rhythm Basics* teaches you the rhythm styles used in traditional and contemporary acoustic guitar music – strum patterns, bass lines, percussive grooves, drones, and more. Whether you're a beginning or an intermediate guitarist, the progressive lessons and accompanying CD will help you to master the fundamentals of rhythm.

_____00695665 Book/CD Pack..........................$16.95

SLIDE BASICS

by David Hamburger

David Hamburger, leading sideman, solo performer and teacher, guides players through this complete introduction to bottleneck slide guitar playing with progressive lessons in open tunings and fingerstyle technique, tips on slide guitars and gear, technical exercises, and full songs.

_____00695610 Book/CD Pack..........................$16.95

SOLO FINGERSTYLE BASICS

Enrich your playing with the expressive, dynamic, symphonic textures of solo fingerstyle guitar. With the guidance of master teachers, you'll learn to build simple melodies into complete guitar arrangements, understand fingerings that will bring intimidating chords within your reach, and put you at ease with country blues, classical techniques, Celtic music and more!

_____00695597 Book/CD Pack..........................$14.95

ACOUSTIC GUITAR ESSENTIALS

ACOUSTIC BLUES GUITAR ESSENTIALS

The 12 "private lessons" in this book/CD pack are full of helpful examples, licks, great songs, and excellent advice on blues flatpicking rhythm and lead, fingerpicking, and slide techniques from some of the finest teachers around, including Mike Christiansen, *Acoustic Guitar* music editor Dylan Shorer, Stefan Grossman and many others. The book shows all examples in both standard notation and tablature.

_____00699186 Book/CD Pack..........................$19.95

ALTERNATE TUNINGS GUITAR ESSENTIALS

Unlock the secrets of playing and composing in alternate tunings. Includes an introduction to alternate tunings and the players who have pioneered them (including tips from David Wilcox, David Crosby, Alex de Grassi, Duncan Sheik and more), 12 in-depth lessons in 11 tunings, 10 full songs to play, a special section on how to create your own tunings, an extensive list of 60 tunings to try – with artist songs and examples, and accessible arrangements in standard notation and tablature.

_____00695557 Book/CD Pack..........................$19.95

FINGERSTYLE GUITAR ESSENTIALS

12 in-depth lessons for players of all levels, taught and recorded by the master teachers at *Acoustic Guitar* magazine. Also includes 8 full songs, including: Ashokan Farewell • If I Only Had a Brain • Satin Doll • and more.

_____00699145 Book/CD Pack..........................$19.95

FLATPICKING GUITAR ESSENTIALS

Learn bluegrass and folk with this book/CD package featuring lessons by *Acoustic Guitar* assistant editor Scott Nygaard, award-winning guitarist Dix Bruce, legendary guitarist Happy Traum, and many others. Includes 16 complete songs to play: Banish Misfortune • Kentucky Waltz • Sally Goodin • Soldier's Joy • Will the Circle Be Unbroken • more.

_____00699174 Book/CD Pack..........................$19.95

SWING GUITAR ESSENTIALS

This comprehensive book/CD pack includes 5 full songs (including "Minor Swing" and "Avalon") and 10 in-depth lessons for players of all levels, taught and recorded (slowly and up to tempo) by the master teachers at *Acoustic Guitar* magazine. It introduces guitarists to swing's essential styles and pioneering players – from Eddie Lang to Count Basie's rhythm master Freddie Green to Hot Club virtuoso Django Reinhardt, and covers topics such as jazz chord basics, moveable chord forms, swing soloing, and more.

_____00699193 Book/CD Pack..........................$19.95

Prices, contents, and availability subject to change without notice.

FOR MORE INFORMATION, SEE YOUR LOCAL MUSIC DEALER, OR WRITE TO:

HAL•LEONARD®
CORPORATION

7777 W. BLUEMOUND RD. P.O. BOX 13819 MILWAUKEE, WI 53213

Visit Hal Leonard Online at **www.halleonard.com**

Hal Leonard Proudly Presents Reference Books from

S T R I N G   L E T T E R   P U B L I S H I N G

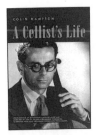

A CELLIST'S LIFE
Strings Backstage Series

One of the 20th century's most distinguished cellists, Colin Hampton, is your guide to a bygone world of classical music and musicians. Through his witty, convivial, and candid narratives, you'll also encounter such luminaries as Pablo Casala, Ernest Bloch, Igor Stravinsky, Arturo Toscanini, Béla Bartók, Yehudi Menuhin, and other as never before.

_____ 00330753 (128 pages, 6" x 9") $12.95

CUSTOM GUITARS
A COMPLETE GUIDE TO CONTEMPORARY HANDCRAFTED GUITARS

This beautiful book is a comprehensive guide to the new Golden Age of handcrafted acoustic guitars! Illustrated with full-color photos of custom instruments throughout, this rich resource also contains profiles of top luthiers, advice on buying a custom instrument, and an extensive directory with complete contact information for hundreds of makers. Encompassing steel-string flattops, nylon-strings, resonators & Hawaiians, archtops and more, *Custom Guitars* presents the history and current state of the art of guitar making. Includes an intro by Alex de Grassi.

_____ 00330564 (150 pages, 9" x 12") $39.95

ROCK TROUBADOURS
by Jeffrey Pepper Rodgers
Acoustic Guitar Backstage Series

In these revealing conversations, today's top artists offer a look inside their creative process as songwriters, guitarists, recording artists and performers. Includes Jerry Garcia and David Grisman, Paul Simon, Joni Mitchell, James Taylor, Ani DiFranco, Dave Matthews and Tim Reynolds, Indigo Girls, Ben Harper, Chris Whitley and more.

_____ 00330752 (128 pages, 6" x 9") $14.95

21ST-CENTURY CELLISTS
Strings Backstage Series

This collection of interviews sparkles with the individual personalities of some of this century's most gifted cellists. With voices as unique as their instruments', these musicians reveal the facets and textures of their professional and personal lives. From the intrepid Bion Tsang to the dynamic Kenneth Slowik and the charming Yo-Yo Ma, these artists and many others discuss what it's like to be a soloist, member of an ensemble, composer, mentor, musical activist and recording artist. How they began, what cultural and historical forces shaped them, how they practice, and what they aspire to – this and more are illuminated in this fascinating volume. Artists include: David Finckel, Ralph Kirshbaum, Laurence Lesser, Yo-Yo Ma, Kermit Moore, Carlos Prieto, Hai-Ye Ni, Kenneth Slowik, Bion Tsang, Jian Wang and Peter Wispelwey.

_____ 00330754 (128 pages, 6" x 9") $14.95

21ST CENTURY STRING QUARTETS, VOL.1
Strings Backstage Series

In this collection of in-depth interviews from the publishers of *Strings* magazine, some of the most talented and inspiring string quartets of our time explain how they work through their personal and musical relationships, from the practice room to the stage.

_____ 00330530 (128 pages, 6" x 9") $12.95

21ST CENTURY VIOLINISTS, VOLUME 1
Strings Backstage Series

A rare glimpse into the fascinating lives of classical violin soloists: how they practice, how they work with other musicians, their performance secrets and anxieties, what moves and inspires them – all this and more comes to life in this series of revealing one-on-one interviews with the writers of *Strings* magazine.

_____ 00699221 (128 pages, 6" x 9") $12.95

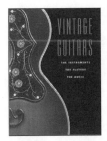

VINTAGE GUITARS
THE INSTRUMENTS, THE PLAYERS, AND THE MUSIC

Vintage Guitars: The Instruments, the Players, and the Music is the first pictorial reference work to offer guitar enthusiasts, players and collectors an opportunity to explore the eventful, endless give-and-take between musicians and instrument makers that has produced America's popular music and its quintessential instrument. Generously illustrated with more than 150 photos of players, instruments, catalog pages and other memorabilia, this book features everything from the elegant American guitars of the 19th century to the evolving dreadnought, jumbo, 12-string, archtop resophonic and more – original instruments as well as contemporary incarnations and reissues. It spotlights the guitars of Leadbelly, Jimmie Rodgers, the Everly Brothers, Tony Rice, Emmylou Harris, Ben Harper and others. The collector's edition features the book in a classy, hard-back slip case.

_____ 00330780 (162 pages, 9" x 12") $39.95

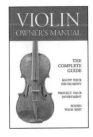

VIOLIN OWNER'S MANUAL

Here's the book that should have come with your violin! Written by a team of leading instrument makers, repairers and musicians, this is the one comprehensive guide to selecting, understanding, preserving and protecting any violin, from a modest fiddle to a priceless Stradivari. Richly illustrated with photographs and drawings, it covers topics including: selecting the proper instrument and bow, understanding common repairs, finding the right maker, guarding against theft, getting a good setup, protecting your violin, choosing a case, and more.

_____ 00330762 (152 pages, 6" x 9") $14.95

VIOLIN VIRTUOSOS
Strings Backstage Series

An exceptional variety of dynamic violin soloists are making their mark on the world's stages. *Violin Virtuosos* takes you into their world. In these compelling profiles, each musician reveals the personal, technical, and psychological aspects of their lives in music: how they cope with isolation, how they approach and interpret their repertoire, and what kindles their passions and unites them with their audiences. This fascinating companion to Vol. 1 includes profiles of Joshua Bell, Vadim Repin, Kyung-Wha Chung, Hilary Hahn, Viktoria Mullova, Leila Josefowicz, Christian Tetzlaff and more.

_____ 00330566 (128 pages, 6" x 9") $12.95

Prices, contents, and availability subject to change without notice.

FOR MORE INFORMATION, SEE YOUR LOCAL MUSIC DEALER,
OR WRITE TO:

HAL•LEONARD®
CORPORATION

7777 W. BLUEMOUND RD. P.O. BOX 13819 MILWAUKEE, WI 53213

Visit Hal Leonard Online at **www.halleonard.com**